T0396785

THE GREAT INDIAN
thali

THE GREAT INDIAN

thali

SEASONAL VEGETARIAN WHOLESOMENESS

TEXT & PHOTOGRAPHS
NANDITA IYER

ILLUSTRATIONS
ABHILASHA DEWAN & ANITA VERMA

Lustre Press
Roli Books

Contents

Introduction

Indian food is plural like none other. The profusion of produce and the climatic, ethnic, religious, and cultural diversity across 3.28 million square kilometres unite to form what is broadly called Indian cuisine.

Apart from India's rich meat-based culinary traditions, its vegetarian cuisine can proudly claim to cover the largest diversity of plant and dairy-based dishes. The Indian kitchen is easily, the go-to source if you are vegetarian, where the cooking and recipes are not *vegetarianized* or *veganized*, but have been so, traditionally, for thousands of years.

What makes some of India's communities vegetarian?

India's unique geography is one of the key influences in its food culture. The Himalayas and the Hindu Kush range in Pakistan block out cold winds coming in from Central Asia, enabling the Indian subcontinent to have a more hospitable weather pattern round the year, which in turn, leads to an incredible variety in fresh, seasonal produce.

Despite this astounding diversity, a few staples are common across the country and make the backbone of its cuisine. Some of these have been grown here for around 6,000–8,000 years. For example, rice (believed to have its origins in China), sugarcane, mango, barley, sorghum, mustard, pepper, turmeric, moong, urad dal, millet, native variety of vegetables like gourds, cluster beans, broad beans, eggplant, and plantains. Milk, yoghurt and ghee have also been integral to Indian cuisine with ample mentions in Vedic literature. *Charaka-samhita*, a medicinal tome written 2,000 years ago describes a bewildering variety of oils, fruits, local grains, vegetables and animal products – many of which continue to be used even today.

A year-round cropping pattern comprising Rabi, Kharif and Zaid crops ensures a plentiful supply of grains, lentils, vegetables, and fruits all through the year for a bulk of India's regions.

Indian cuisine was made richer by confluences, migration, different ruling empires, trade, and colonialism. Indian cooking too, has changed gradually but considerably over the last 500 to 600 years.

Exotic spices like black pepper, cinnamon, cardamom and nutmeg drew the Arabs, Portuguese, Spanish, Dutch, and British alike to our lands. It is fascinating to think of how present-day staples like potatoes, tomatoes, chillies, peanuts, corn, and beans were introduced to India only around 300 years ago due to the Columbian Exchange. Some of the other ingredients that came to India via the Columbian Exchange are amaranth (rajgira), cashews, chayote squash, pumpkin, sunflower, maize, peanuts, pineapple, guava, tapioca, and sweet potato.

The transfer, domestication and cultivation of these newer varieties of crops, including beans, vegetables and fruits, added to the possibilities of a vegetarian diet in India. With the coming of the Mughals in 1526 came elaborate meat recipes, kormas, kebabs, biryani and the addition of saffron, fruits, nuts, and cream in dishes. Curries with rich gravies and using the tandoor for cooking was also a Mughal influence. Although this was largely meat-based, many of these ingredients and techniques are used in present-day 'Punjabi' or 'North-West Frontier Province' cooking in restaurants, even when it comes to vegetarian dishes. The tandoor is still used to make a variety of breads and kebabs in restaurants.

How did India turn to vegetarianism?

Vegetarianism in India is around 2,500 years old. It became popular after the advent of Jainism and Buddhism in the sixth century BCE. These faiths, which sought to compete with the prevailing Vedic faith, introduced ahimsa (non-violence) to mainstream Vedic belief, which otherwise was rather meat-heavy, although some puranas, presumably composed later, do recommend vegetarianism as an ideal to pursue.

The Aryans, who were pastoralists, gradually started settling in the Gangetic plains stretching all the way up to modern-day Bangladesh. The *Upanishads* (which are commentaries on the Vedas), *Manusmriti* (a book of laws that outlines the caste system), and Krishna's teachings in the *Bhagavad Gita*, all sing the virtues of vegetarianism, in a slow and gradual change from the original and older Rig Vedic focus on ritualistic animal sacrifices.

Over the years, most Brahmins and trading communities in India veered towards vegetarianism. The formalization of the varna/caste system around 2,000 years ago also made food habits a core part of every caste and subcaste's identity. Until rather recently, because of stringent caste-centric food habits, the phenomenon of eating out was a rarity for upper-caste communities.

Some vegetarian communities are stricter than the rest in even avoiding onions and garlic in their food. The priest class in most communities follow a strict vegetarian diet in some of India's regions. Jainism is probably the faith that advocates the harshest of vegetarianisms, with a long list of foods to be abstained from and the year punctuated with many fasting days.

Ayurveda classifies food based on their yogic qualities (guna) into sattvic, rajasic and tamasic, and recommends a sattvic diet for wellness and good health. A sattvic diet incorporates the principles of ahimsa, and is believed to be energizing and conscious compared to the rajasic and tamasic that are stimulating and sedating, respectively. Dairy is allowed to be a part of a sattvic diet when cows have been treated ethically and if milk is collected only after the calf has had its fill.

What does the produce of vegetarian diet look like?

Grains and flours: Wheat, rice, barley, millets as whole grains, flours and fermented batters.
Lentils and beans: Tur dal, moong dal, chana dal and masoor dal are the four most commonly used dals, used as whole, split, skinned and or as flour. Chickpeas, kidney

beans, green moong, black eyed peas are few of the large variety of legumes used in Indian cooking.

Vegetables and fruits: Vegetables are prepared as stir-fries, curries with sauces, in combination with lentils or legumes, added to rice to make pulaos and to flour to make parathas, made into chutneys and even desserts. Seasonal fruits are eaten on their own or as part of a dessert or even a curry. Vegetables and fruits are both made into pickles and preserves as well.

Dairy: In India, the term vegetarian by default means lacto-vegetarian. Dairy products like milk, yoghurt, cream, butter, buttermilk, paneer, and ghee are used liberally in the daily diet. Paneer is more prevalent in the dairy belt of India, in states like Punjab and Haryana.

Spices: Spices add flavour to food along with health benefits. In Indian cuisine, spices are not just used in savoury dishes but also in sweets.

Oils: Oils are used for sautéing spices, masalas, and vegetables. They are used in the all-important tadka or tempering that adds a finishing touch to most savoury dishes and also for deep-frying. Traditionally, ghee, coconut oil, sesame oil (gingelly), mustard oil, and groundnut oil are some of the main cooking mediums although in present times, neutral flavoured oils like rice bran, sunflower, and soybean oils are regularly used.

Nuts and seeds: Besides oil extraction, seeds are used in tempering or as a garnish. They are also used to thicken gravies and in snacks.

Festivals, feasts, temples

Shrines across the country serve a special prasad or a meal that it is well known for, such as the langar in the Golden Temple, Amritsar; banana leaf meal in Udupi, or the Tirupati laddoo prasadam.

How is a thali designed?

The main meal in a vegetarian household is usually centred around a starch component, be it rice, wheat or millets. Steamed rice, khichdi, rice-based breads, rotis, parathas, millets, steamed dumplings of millets (ragi mudde) are all the different ways in which a carbohydrate forms the centre of the meal. This is eaten with vegetable-based curries (prepared dry or in a gravy), dal, legumes, green leafy vegetables, buttermilk or yoghurt-based dishes – all of which form the side dishes. A full thali has four to five such side dishes that are eaten with roti and/or rice. There are also a number of condiments, either preserves or prepared fresh in the cuisine of each community. Green chutney, red chilli and garlic chutney, and pickles are some examples of condiments. Fruits are used to prepare sweets or served along with the meal, for example, banana at the end of a Kerala sadhya.

No special days or festivals are complete without a sweet dish. These are either milk-based puddings (kheer/payasam/payesh), or flour, ghee and sugar made into a halwa, or solidified milk-based sweets. There are also steamed sweets offered as prasad such as modak for Ganesh Chaturthi.

Deconstructing the thali

A thali is a coming together of thousands of years of civilizations, societies, world trade, migration, invasion, domestication of crops, agriculture and seasons, all of this accommodated in a circle of twelve inches diameter or less.

A thali is a large metal dish with raised sides. While the dry items are laid directly on the thali, small cups/bowls are used to serve dishes like dal, rasam, and kheer. Thalis can be made out of any metal, even gold and silver! Bengali and Assamese thalis are made of bell metal or kansa.

A complete Indian meal combines the six known basic flavours and a variety of textures. Except for Bengali cuisine, it is all served together and not course wise. A banana leaf is regularly used to serve full meals in the South. Dividing the leaf into the upper deck and lower deck, everything has a place on the leaf. Care is taken as to what is served on the right, left, up and down, keeping in mind that the person is eating with her right hand. In *Feasts and Fasts: A History of Food in India*, author Colleen Taylor Sen explains how broths, water, drinks, food that is sucked and licked, and pickles are always served on the left, be it in the thali or a banana leaf. Onam Sadhya is a grand example of a South Indian vegetarian meal. In Manipur, plates and cups are stitched out of leaves. The components of a thali differ from region to region and with the seasons.

A betel leaf preparation (paan) may be served at the end of the meal. The leaf itself along with the fillings make an excellent digestive.

Types of vegetarian food in India

From homes to temples and gurdwaras, street fare to gourmet cuisine in high-end restaurants, from Kashmir to Kanyakumari, India offers the widest variety of vegetarian dishes like no other country in the world.

Everyday home cooking – Ghar ka khana

What we cook at home every day depends on our culture, family preferences, availability of ingredients, prices, seasonal produce and so on. These meals are usually economical, fuss-free and quick to prepare. Ghar ka khana also includes repurposing leftovers into tasty snacks and meals.

Street food

Street food is specific to every micro geography in India. Its hyperlocal nature means there is no requirement or need to transport ingredients from faraway places. This helps keep the logistics simple and the food affordable. It is often freshly made and served due to no access to refrigeration or preservation. You will find that a lot many street foods are deep-fried or have deep-fried components as it is the quickest way of cooking – for example, chaat. Dhabas along highways are another example of delicious vegetarian food on the go. Vaishnav dhabas are pure vegetarian, where food is prepared fresh every day.

Restaurant food

Eating out at vegetarian-only restaurants in India is quite popular. The one drawback of eating in meat-based restaurants is that vegetarian dishes often feature a very limited range of main ingredients such as paneer and potatoes with not much importance given to creating dishes with the wide array of produce available.

In *The Great Indian Thali*, you will find a taste of vegetarian dishes from different parts of India grouped by the seasons – spring, summer, monsoon, and winter; from the globally popular to the humble home-cooked fare, each one of them heart-warming at its core.

Glossary

Amaranth flour / Rajgira – Amaranth flour is a gluten-free, protein rich flour made from the seeds of the amaranth plant.

Asafoetida / Hing – Asafoetida is a sulphurous smelling resin that comes from the Ferula plant. It is traditionally ground into a powder and used as a spice to add a savoury, garlic-like flavour to food.

Barnyard millet – The wild seed of a fast-growing crop, barnyard millet is a fibre-rich grain whose taste is very similar to that of broken rice, thus making it a suitable replacement for the health-conscious.

Bitter gourd / Karela – A vegetable of the gourd family with warty green skin that has a strong bitter taste and multiple health benefits such as blood sugar control and weight loss.

Black gram / Urad dal (with skin/skinned/split/whole) – A widely used pulse in the Indian subcontinent whose whole black version has a unique mucilaginous texture that lends thickness to dal preparations while the dehusked, white version is used to make idli and dosa, and the split version is used in South Indian tadkas.

Black salt / Kala namak – A kiln fired rock salt with a sulphurous and pungent smell that comes from its sulphur content and is a key component of chaat masala that is used to flavour street food in North India.

Cardamom / Elaichi (green/black) – Cardamom is a spice that comes from multiple plants in the ginger family. The green variety has an intensely aromatic, resinous fragrance while the black one has a distinctly more smoky aroma.

Carom seed / Ajwain – These seeds come from a herb in the cumin and parsley family and has a sharp and penetrating flavour. It is used both in traditional medicine as well as in the kitchen.

Chaat masala – A popular spice mix of amchoor (dried mango powder), cumin, coriander, dried ginger, black salt, black pepper, asafoetida (hing), and chilli powder that is sprinkled on fruit salads and street food.

Chilli powder – It is the pulverized powder of dried chillies of various varieties. The Kashmiri chilli produces a low-heat, high-colour powder that is used to lend a bright red colour to food while other varieties lend more heat.

Cluster beans – Also called Guar, it's a legume that produces clusters of pods whose seeds contain a very powerful gelling agent that is used as a thickener. The pods themselves are cooked as a vegetable.

Coconut / Nariyal (fresh, desiccated, frozen) – The fruit of the Coconut palm and the grated fresh white flesh of the fruit is used regularly in South Indian cooking. The flesh can also be dessicated before being grated to improve its shelf life.

Colocasia / Arbi (root, leaf) – Is a starchy root vegetable with soft, easily-digestible white flesh that can be boiled, roasted, or fried. The leaves of the plant are also edible and are used to make the Gujarati snack, patra.

CTC tea – Crush, tear, curl is a method of processing black tea in which the leaves are passed through a series of cylindrical rollers with sharp teeth that crush, tear, and curl the tea into small, hard pellets that produces a strong and intense tea flavour.

Custard apple – Also known as Sitaphal or Sugar Apple, it is a segmented fruit with white flesh surrounding multiple seeds and has a custard-like texture and flavour.

Dried white peas / Vatana – These are produced by harvesting fully mature green peas and drying them. Since fresh green peas are not available all through the year, this is a suitable alternative.

Drumstick (Moringa) / Sahjan – The fruit of the Moringa tree, this 30-40 cm long fibrous pod contains multiple fleshy seeds that are boiled/steamed and eaten. The leaves of the tree are also edible.

Fenugreek / Methi (seed, leaves) – Yellowish brown seeds with a strong aromatic profile that are used to flavour dishes all over the subcontinent. The leaf of the plant is also edible and is used both fresh as well as dried (kasuri methi).

Foxtail millet – One of the oldest grains consumed in the Indian subcontinent, this millet is a drought-resistant crop that lends the grain a dense nutritional profile rich in gluten-free protein and other micronutrients.

Fried gram / Dalia – Dalia is roasted chana dal that has a nutty aroma and powdery texture that makes it a low-cost replacement for more expensive nuts.

Garam masala powder – A blend of ground spices that is used as a finishing spice mix for dishes in the Indian subcontinent. It is typically made from a blend of bay leaves, black pepper, clove, cinnamon, cardamom, coriander, fennel, and cumin.

Gram flour / Besan – A pulse flour made from the ground Bengal gram. It is rich in both starch and gluten-free protein and is used as a starch binder.

Gingelly oil – Another name for edible vegetable oil derived from sesame seeds. One of the subcontinent's earliest cooking oils, it has a distinctive nutty aroma that makes it a flavour enhancer in many Asian cuisines.

Horsegram – A drought-resistant legume that has been grown in the Indian subcontinent for over 5,000 years, horse gram needs to be soaked and cooked for long periods of time to be palatable.

Ivy gourd / Tindora / Tendli – An edible vegetable of the gourd family that looks like baby cucumbers and can be deep fried, sautéed, or steamed.

Jaggery / Gur – Jaggery is a traditional form of sugar consumed in the Indian subcontinent. It is a concentrated product of sugarcane juice without separation of molasses and crystals thus lending it a colour that varies from golden brown to dark brown. Jaggery can also be made from date or palm sap.

Khoya – Is a dairy food widely used in Indian cuisines made of either dried whole milk or milk thickened by heating in an open iron pan.

Long beans – A legume with long, edible green pods containing immature seeds that is consumed as a vegetable.

Manipuri black rice – A glutinous (sticky) variety of rice from Northeast India with high amounts of fibre and anti-oxidants.

Maida / Refined flour / All-purpose flour – Maida is a white wheat flour from the Indian subcontinent. It is finely milled without any bran, refined, and bleached. Maida is used extensively for making fast foods, baked goods such as pastries, bread, several varieties of sweets, and traditional flatbreads such as naan or kulcha.

Mustard oil – Mustard oil is a vegetable oil produced from mustard seeds and has a strong, pungent aroma that lends cuisines that use it their characteristic flavour. Heating the oil until it smokes before using it for cooking reduces its pungency.

Nigella seeds – Also called kalonji, these black coloured seeds have a subtle, onion-like flavour.

Papad – A seasoned flatbread made from the dried dough of black gram flour that is typically fried or cooked over dry heat until crunchy. Papads can also be made from lentils, chickpeas, rice, tapioca, millets or potato flours.

Panch phoron – A whole spice blend from eastern India that typically contains these seeds: mustard, cumin, fennel, celery, and fenugreek.

Pav – A soft and fluffy bread roll introduced by the Portuguese to coastal Goa and Maharashtra that gets its soft texture from the use of milk and milk powder in the dough.

Pav Bhaji masala – A special spice mix used to prepare Mumbai's famous street food. A combination of many whole spices and spice powders, it is best to buy a pack of this instead of making it at home.

Pointed gourd / Parwal – This vegetable belongs to the cucumber family, widely cultivated in the eastern and some northern parts of India.

Poppy seed – An oilseed obtained from the poppy plant, these off white coloured seeds are popular in Bengali cooking. Called posto, the seeds are soaked and ground to a paste and used in several dishes.

Ragi flour / Finger millet flour – Ground finger millets gives ragi flour. The millets are sometimes soaked, sprouted, sun dried and then ground to get a more nutritious ragi flour. This flour is naturally gluten free.

Raw mango powder / Amchoor – Tart raw mangoes are peeled, sliced and sun dried. The dried mango pieces are ground to a powder, which is called amchoor. It is pale brown in colour with a sour flavour. Amchoor is used in dry curries for adding sourness without extra moisture.

Rasam powder – This is a spice mix made from roasted and powdered dals and spices. Rasam is usually a thin broth made using a dal water stock. This aromatic rasam powder adds both flavour and a bit of thickness to the rasam.

Rava / Sooji – Also known as semolina, it is coarse and purified milled durum wheat that is used to make upma and sweet dishes in the Indian subcontinent.

Ridge gourd / Torai – In India, ridge gourd is cultivated as a vegetable. When it is allowed to mature and ripen fully, the inside of the gourd turns completely fibrous, making it into a loofah or scrubbing sponge. Ridge gourd is made into mild curries, chutneys, and even fried snacks. The peels of ridge gourd can also be used to make chutneys.

Rock salt – Salt mined from mineral deposits from ancient evaporated lakes and seas. This salt usually contains minerals other than sodium chloride thus lending it slightly different colours and flavours. Himalayan pink salt is one kind of rock salt.

Sesame seeds, white – Called til in Hindi and ellu in Tamil, Malayalam and Kannada, these nutty and fragrant seeds are said to have originated in India and domesticated over 3,000 years ago. It is used in tempering, to add a crunch to dough, in spice mixes, and also in sweets.

Sev – These are noodles of varying thickness made from gram flour (besan) and deep fried. Thicker varieties of sev are served as a snack on their own. The finer varieties are used in chaat dishes such as bhel puri, sev puri, and ragda patties as a garnish.

Sorghum flour / Jowar atta – Sorghum or jowar is a summer millet. It is usually used in Indian cooking as a flour to make rotis, which are naturally gluten free. It can also be made into a porridge and other snack like dishes such as muthia.

Subzi – While subzi means vegetable in Hindi (subzi-mandi meaning vegetable market), it is also a terminology for a dry vegetable preparation. For example: aloo ki subzi meaning a dry potato dish.

Tamarind (pods, paste, extract) / Imli – Tamarind is a leguminous tree that produces an abundance of brown pod-like fruits. Each pod has a tangy pulp and seeds. The mature fruit has a sweet-sour balance. Tamarind is sold as compressed pods and paste. The pods are soaked in hot water for 15 -30 minutes and squeezed to get tamarind extract.

Tava – It is a commonly used utensil in India, either flat or concave, used to make all kinds of flat breads. A tava can be made of cast iron, aluminium, terracotta, stone, and many other materials depending on the region.

Tempering / Tadka – It is a cooking technique used in the Indian subcontinent where whole spices and at times, fresh ingredients like ginger, garlic, or curry leaves are fried in oil or ghee. It could be done at the start of the cooking process or at the end, to add a final layer of flavour to the dish.

Tempering ladle – It is the small pan used for the final tempering of a dish. Due to the small quantity of oil or ghee required for this purpose, it makes practical sense not to use another large pan for the tempering.

Turmeric / Haldi (fresh root) – Fresh turmeric is a bright orange root, similar to fresh ginger. It is soft enough to be sliced or grated. The fresh root is available in India in the months of December and January. It can be stored in the fridge for up to two weeks and in the freezer for up to six months.

Whole wheat flour / Atta – Atta is a wholemeal wheat flour from the Indian subcontinent that is used to make flatbreads such as chapathi, puri, and paratha.

Yellow moong dal – This is dehusked and split whole green moong, which is yellow on the inside. Yellow moong is one of the commonly used ingredients to make dal. Being a small sized lentil, it cooks quickly as compared to tur dal and chana dal. It is one of the favoured dals to make khichdi.

Basic Recipes

Steamed Rice

TIME TAKEN: 30 MINUTES | SERVES 3-4

Rice is an important and constant feature in any Indian thali. Steamed rice provides a neutral backdrop to enjoy the flavours of dals and curries. Indian cooking uses a large number of rice varieties, basmati being just one of them. The quantity of water required to cook the rice and its eventual texture depends on the variety and the age of the rice. Aged rice absorbs more water and is fluffier when cooked, while new rice absorbs less water and is stickier on cooking. Rice is typically not salted because its accompaniments already have salt and spices.

Ingredients

1 cup (220 g) white rice (dry)

Method

1. Rinse the rice 2-3 times until all the surface starch is washed out and the water is clear.
2. Rice cooker: Place rice in a rice cooker and add 2 cups of water. Switch on the 'cook' mode. The rice cooker turns off automatically when the rice is done.
3. Stovetop: Place the rinsed rice in a pan and add 2 cups of water. Once the water comes to a boil, cover with a lid leaving a small gap to allow the steam to pass through (so that the water does not boil over). Once the water is nearly absorbed, (3-4 minutes after it starts to boil), turn the heat to low and cover with a lid fully. In another 5-7 minutes, the rice should be cooked. Turn off the heat but leave the pan covered for another 15 minutes. Open and fluff the rice with a fork before serving.
4. Pressure Cooker: Add an inch of water (roughly ½ litre) in a pressure cooker. Place the rinsed rice in a container that fits inside the pressure cooker. Add 2 cups of water to the rice. Place the container with the rice in the pressure cooker. Close the lid of the cooker with the weight on, and cook over high heat. Allow to come to full pressure (one whistle). Reduce the heat to low and simmer for 5 minutes. Turn off the heat and allow the pressure to release naturally.
5. You can also cook rice in microwave cookers and in an instant pot.
6. Do note that different kinds of rice have varying cooking times. When cooking rice that takes longer to cook, it is good to make a large batch and either refrigerate or freeze for more than one use.

Phulka

Phulka or roti is one of the commonly made flatbreads in Indian households. A nutritious accompaniment made of stone ground whole wheat flour (chakki atta) and water, you can also add a spoonful of oil to smoothen the dough in the final stage of kneading to prevent it from drying. Making perfectly round and thin phulkas that puff up like balloons needs practice, but it is very doable!

Ingredients

1 cup (120 g) whole wheat flour (atta)
Less than ½ cup luke warm water
1 tsp oil
½ cup extra flour for rolling (atta or rice flour)

Method

1. Take the atta in a large bowl. Make a well in the centre and add the water.
2. Using a wooden spatula or your fingers, work the water into the flour to make a rough dough. Knead gently to fold all the flour into the dough. You may need to add extra spoonfuls of water to get a smooth and soft dough.
3. Add oil and knead a few more times. Make a smooth dough ball and cover with a lid or a damp kitchen towel for 15-30 minutes.
4. Divide the dough into 8 equal portions. If you prefer smaller rotis, divide the dough into 10 or 12 portions.
5. Using your palms, roll each portion into a smooth ball. Use your fingers to press and flatten the ball into a disc.
6. On a clean and even surface or board, sprinkle some flour. Coat the disc in dry flour and place it on the board. Using a rolling pin, roll it out into a thin circle. Sprinkle dry flour or dip the roti in flour in between the rolling process to make sure it does not stick to the board.
7. Place the tava or griddle over high heat. Once the tava is moderately hot, place the rolled roti on it. Cook one side for 10-12 seconds until you see bubbles on the surface. Flip it and cook for another 7-8 seconds. Remove the tava from the heat, pick up the roti using tongs and place it directly over the high flame. The roti will puff up like a balloon. If it does not puff completely, remove from the flame in 2-3 seconds as you don't want it to burn. Non-puffed rotis taste as good.
8. Serve the rotis immediately or wrap them in a muslin cloth to keep warm.

Paratha

Paratha is made using stone ground, whole wheat flour. A plain paratha, without filling, has two or more layers and is sturdier than a phulka. You can make many varieties of parathas by adding spices and herbs in the dough such as kasuri methi, carom seeds, black pepper, and red chilli powder as well as fillings using potatoes, cauliflower, paneer, or mince meat.

Ingredients

2 cups (240 g) whole wheat flour (atta)
1 tbsp + 1 tsp oil
¾ cup water
Ghee or oil to make the parathas
Extra flour to roll out parathas

Method

1. In a large bowl, mix the flour and 1 tbsp oil. Make a well in the centre and add the water. Using a wooden spatula or your fingers, work the water into the flour to make a rough dough. Knead gently to fold in all the flour adding a splash of water occassionally to make a smooth and soft dough.
2. Add 1 tsp oil and knead a few more times. Place the dough in a bowl and cover with a lid for 30 minutes.
3. Divide the dough into 8 portions. Roll each portion into a smooth ball and flatten into a thick disc.
4. Spread some dry flour in a shallow dish. Take one of the discs, coat it with dry flour, and place it on a rolling board or flat, clean surface. Using a rolling pin, roll the disc out into a 4-5" diameter circle. Using the back of a spoon, smear ½ tsp of ghee or oil on the surface. Fold the rolled out disc in half and smear ¼ tsp of ghee on the folded surface. Fold this in half again to make a quarter of a circle. Coat this folded piece in a bit of dry flour. Place it on the board and roll into a triangle or a circle around 6-7" in diameter.
5. Place this on a moderately hot tava or skillet. Once you see bubbles forming on the surface and the top layer of the paratha puffing, flip it over. Apply little ghee or oil on the surface facing up. Using a spatula, press down gently. This process helps in separating out the layers. Cook this side for 30 seconds or so. Once golden brown spots appear, flip over again and apply some ghee or oil to the surface. Remove paratha and repeat the process for the remaining parathas.
6. Serve the paratha immediately or allow to cool for 5 minutes and then stack in a muslin lined roti box. Leftover parathas make great breakfast with scrambled eggs or Indian style pickles.

Idli and Dosa Batter

SOAKING AND FERMENTING TIME: 13 HOURS; TIME TAKEN 15-20 MINUTES |
MAKES AROUND 10 CUPS BATTER

This is a staple meal prep in most South Indian homes. You will find a box of fermented batter stored in the fridge through the week to make a variety of breakfast dishes or quick meals like idli, dosa, uthapam, paniyaram, bonda, etc. Most homes will have a special stone grinder to make the batter, but a regular mixer/blender also works well.

Ingredients

3 cups (650 g) rice (short grain is good)
1 cup (200 g) dehusked black gram
 (whole urad dal)
2 tsp fenugreek seeds
2 tsp salt

Method

1. Wash and soak the rice for 4-5 hours in plenty of water.
2. Wash and soak the urad dal along with fenugreek seeds for 1-2 hours.
3. Drain the soaked rice and place in a blender along with ½ cup of water. Grind to a slightly coarse paste. Scrape this out into a large bowl.
4. Take the drained urad dal and fenugreek seeds in the blender along with another ½ cup water and blend until you get a smooth airy mixture. Scrape it out and add it to the rice batter.
5. Add salt to this batter and mix well with your hands for around 5 minutes. This important step introduces the wild yeast and bacteria to the batter from your skin and aids in fermentation. Cover the bowl with a dish and not an airtight lid. Keep it in a warm place in the kitchen. During the winter, you can keep the batter covered with a towel or blanket or inside the oven with the light turned on for extra warmth to aid fermentation.
6. If the room temperature is around 30°C, fermentation will take around 8 hours. The batter will rise well (almost double in volume) with a lot of bubbles when you stir it with a ladle. At this point, it can be used to make idlis or dosas. At this stage, you can also refrigerate the batter until you are ready to use it.
7. Make sure you remove the batter from the fridge well in advance to bring it back to room temperature before using it to cook.

Dal

Tur dal is the most commonly used dal in everyday cooking. This basic dal recipe can be made into dal fry, or dal tadka, or other variations such as Gujarati dal, Tamilian koottu, sambar, and rasam. Soaking the dal for 30 minutes to an hour helps in the cooking process.

Ingredients

1 cup (200 g) split pigeon peas (tur dal)
¼ tsp ground turmeric
½ tsp oil

Method

1. Rinse the dal 2-3 times. Soak in a bowl of water for 30 minutes to an hour.
2. Drain the soaked dal and place in a pressure cooker. Add 2 cups water, turmeric and oil. The oil prevents the dal from frothing during the process of the pressure release (whistle).
3. Close the lid along with the weight on. Allow to come to full pressure (one whistle) over high heat. Reduce the heat to low and cook for 12 minutes. Turn off the heat and allow the pressure to release naturally.
4. Open the lid and whisk the dal well for a smooth consistency. Skip this step if you prefer your dal with more texture.

Kachumbar

Onion Tomato Cucumber Salad

TIME TAKEN: 15 MINUTES | SERVES 4

A couple of spoons of this salad adds freshness to any Indian thali.

Ingredients

1 large cucumber
1 medium onion
1 large tomato
½ tsp salt
1 lemon
¼ tsp red chilli powder (optional)
1 tbsp finely chopped fresh coriander leaves

Method

1. Peel the cucumber and onion and cut them into fine dice. Chop the tomato finely.
2. In a small bowl, combine the chopped vegetables.
3. Add the salt, juice of lemon, red chilli powder, and toss well.
4. Garnish with fresh coriander.
5. Refrigerate until ready to serve.

Sambar

This South Indian staple is prepared using dal and seasonal vegetables. Onion, pumpkin, lady's finger, carrot, brinjal are commonly used singly or combined.

Ingredients

2 tsp oil
2 cups chopped vegetables of choice [not given in grams, this depends on the veggies used]
2 tsp tamarind paste or
  1 cup light tamarind extract
1 cup water (if using tamarind paste) +
  ½ cup water
1½ tsp salt
½ tsp ground turmeric
1 tbsp sambar powder
3 cups cooked tur dal (see page 27)

TEMPERING
2 tsp oil
1 sprig curry leaves
2 dried red chillies
¼ tsp fenugreek seeds
½ tsp black mustard seeds
Pinch of asafoetida

Method

1. In a deep, heavy-bottomed pan, heat the oil. Sauté the vegetables over medium heat for 2-3 minutes.
2. Add the tamarind paste (along with 1 cup water) or the tamarind extract, salt and turmeric. Bring to a boil.
3. Reduce the heat and simmer for 7-8 minutes until the raw smell of tamarind is gone and the vegetables are cooked (the time may vary depending on the type of vegetables you use).
4. Mix the sambar powder in ½ cup water, and add it to the pan. Let it come to a boil.
5. Whisk the cooked dal until smooth and transfer it to the pan. Bring to a gentle simmer. Adjust the consistency of the sambar to that of thick soup.
6. For the tempering, heat the oil in a small pan. Add all the tempering ingredients. As soon as the mustard seeds splutter, transfer the tempering over the sambar. Serve with hot rice, idlis, or dosas.

Dal Fry

This is a basic dal recipe that is often found in dhabas in North India, served with freshly made tandoori rotis. Tur dal works best for dal fry, although a small portion of chana dal can be mixed for added texture.

Ingredients

2 tbsp ghee
Pinch of asafoetida
2 dried red chillies
1 tsp cumin seeds
4-5 cloves garlic, chopped
1 tsp grated ginger
1 medium sized onion, thinly sliced
2 medium sized tomatoes, diced
1 tsp salt
1 tsp red chilli powder
3 cups cooked split pigeon peas (tur dal, see page 27), (cooked with turmeric)
1 tsp kasuri methi
2 tbsp finely chopped coriander leaves

Method

1. Heat the ghee in a large pan.
2. Fry the asafoetida, red chillies, and cumin seeds. Once the cumin seeds sizzle, add the ginger and garlic. Sauté on medium heat for 30 seconds.
3. Add the sliced onions and sauté for 7-8 minutes until it is softened.
4. Add the chopped tomatoes and salt. Cook over high heat until tomatoes are pulpy.
5. Stir in the red chilli powder. Add the cooked dal and bring to a simmer.
6. In the final stage, sprinkle crushed kasuri methi. Transfer to a serving bowl and garnish with fresh coriander. Serve hot with rice or rotis.

Dhansak Masala

Ingredients

5-6 dried red chillies (mild)
1 tsp cumin seeds
1 tbsp coriander seeds
2 pieces of 1" cinnamon sticks
2 green cardamoms
6 black peppercorns

Method

1. Buy this readymade masala or else grind it fresh. Dry roast dried red chillies (mild), cumin seeds, coriander seeds, cinnamon sticks, green cardamoms, and peppercorns until aromatic and grind to a fine powder.

Moong Dal

This is a light dal that is quick to cook. It is suitable for a simple dinner of rice and a vegetable dish. It can be made heartier by adding greens like spinach.

Ingredients

1 cup (200 g) split yellow moong dal
½ tsp ground turmeric
½ tsp oil
1 tbsp ghee
1 bay leaf
1 tsp cumin seeds
3-4 cloves garlic, chopped
½ tsp grated ginger
1 medium sized tomato, chopped
1 tsp red chilli powder
1 tsp salt
2-3 tbsp chopped coriander

Method

1. Rinse and soak the dal for 15 minutes.
2. Drain and place in a deep pan with 2 cups water, turmeric, and oil. Bring to a boil and lower the heat.
3. Skim off the froth that forms on the surface. Cook for 15 minutes until the dal is cooked.
4. While the dal is cooking, prepare the tempering. Heat the ghee in a large pan. Add the bay leaf and cumin seeds. Once the cumin seeds sizzle, add the garlic and ginger. Sauté for 2-3 minutes. Add the chopped tomatoes, red chilli powder, and salt. Cook until the tomatoes are pulpy.
5. Transfer the cooked dal to this pan and stir to combine. Thin with some hot water if needed and bring to a simmer. Remove from heat and garnish with fresh coriander. Serve with rice or rotis.

- *You can prepare masoor dal or pink lentils similarly.*

Khichdi

Khichdi is soul food for most Indians. It can be prepared using any combination of grains and pulses. There's a saying in Hindi that goes 'Khichdi ke chaar yaar – dahi, papad, ghee, aur achaar', translated in English it means, khichdi has four friends – yoghurt, papad, ghee, and pickles. That's how a humble meal can be elevated with simple condiments already in your pantry. Learn to cook a good khichdi and you're never far away from a comforting bowl of food. It is also good for babies, elderly, and those convalescing.

Ingredients

$2/3$ cup (150 g) rice
$1/3$ cup (75 g) split yellow moong dal
3½ / 4 cups water
1 tsp salt
¼ tsp ground turmeric
1 tsp oil or ghee

TEMPERING
1 tbsp ghee
1 tsp cumin seeds
3-4 cloves garlic, sliced (optional)
½ tsp grated ginger
1 green chilli, sliced

Method

1. Rinse the rice and dal. Soak together in a bowl of water for 30 minutes.
2. Drain the soaked rice and dal.
3. Place in a pressure cooker with 3½/4 cups of water. Add the salt, turmeric and 1 tsp ghee.
4. Stir well and close the pressure cooker lid. Allow to come to full pressure over high heat (one whistle).
5. Reduce the heat to low, and then to sim and continue to cook for 8-10 minutes.
6. Turn off the heat and let the pressure drop naturally.
7. Open the lid and mash the khichdi with the back of a ladle. Transfer to a bowl.
8. Heat the ghee for tempering in a small pan. Add all the tempering ingredients. Remove before the garlic turns brown. Transfer the prepared tempering over the khichdi and serve it hot with your choice of accompaniment.

- Lentils like split green gram (moong), tur dal, and masoor dal can be used instead of moong dal.
- Chopped mixed vegetables like carrot, potato, cauliflower can be added to the rice and dal in the cooker.

Green Chutney

A useful condiment that pairs well with many Indian snacks and breakfast dishes.

Ingredients

2 cups (100 g) chopped fresh coriander leaves
1 cup (16 g) chopped mint leaves
3-4 green chillies
2 cloves garlic, peeled
½ tsp grated ginger
2 tbsp fried gram
1 tsp salt
1 tsp sugar
1 tbsp lime juice
¼ tsp ground turmeric
¼ cup water

Method

1. Add all the ingredients to a blender jar along with ¼ cup water and blend to a fine puree. Transfer to an airtight glass jar and refrigerate. This will stay good for a week. Use as an accompaniment to your meals or to make sandwiches.

Instant Tamarind Chutney

TIME TAKEN: UNDER 10 MINUTES | MAKES ½ CUP

Ingredients

3 tbsp (45 g) tamarind paste
¼ cup (40 g) grated jaggery
½ tsp salt*
½ tsp ground cumin
¼ tsp ground dried ginger (sonth)
¼ tsp black salt

Method

1. In a pan, combine tamarind paste and jaggery. Place over medium heat. Bring this to a boil.
2. Reduce the heat and add salt, ground cumin, ground ginger, and black salt.
3. Simmer for 3-4 minutes until the chutney is thick and syrupy.

Tamarind paste usually has some salt in it, so check and adjust the amount of salt accordingly.

Ginger Paste

Ginger paste is handy to have at home as a lot of Indian recipes call for it. You can also use ginger paste to make ginger tea. Make a small quantity at a time if keeping in the refrigerator. Freezing gives the paste a longer shelf life.

Ingredients

100 grams fresh ginger
2 tbsp water

Method

1. Scrub and wash the ginger well. Peel the skin and cut into small pieces. Using a mixer jar grind to a fine paste along with water. Save in a clean, dry airtight glass bottle in the refrigerator. Use within one week.

Ginger-Garlic Paste

TIME TAKEN: 5 MINUTES | MAKES AROUND 200 GRAMS

Ginger-garlic paste is another common ingredient used in Indian dishes. Having a ready batch in the fridge cuts down on prep time. Use equal quantities of ginger and garlic to make the paste. If the ginger is very strong, use 1 part ginger with 2 parts garlic to make the paste.

Ingredients

100 grams peeled garlic
100 grams ginger
3-4 tbsp water
1 tsp salt
1 tbsp oil

Method

1. Chop the garlic.
2. Scrub and wash the ginger well. Peel the skin and cut into small pieces.
3. Add garlic, ginger, water, and salt to a mixer jar. Grind to a fine paste. Mix in the oil and store in a clean, dry airtight glass jar in the refrigerator. Use within one to two weeks.

SPRiNG

The romance of springtime (*basant ritu*) when nature puts on a show is written about extensively in Indian poetry and features regularly in the songs in Hindustani classical music.

Spring is not a lasting season in most parts of India except the alpine regions. In parts of Himachal Pradesh, apple and plum orchards are in full bloom. The Valley of Flowers in Uttarakhand is a riot of colour as the name suggests, in this season. In the rest of India, spring is but a brief transition between winter and summer around the months of February, March, and April. In the cities, it mostly seems to last just for a couple of weeks before the summer heat takes charge.

Springtime is a season of new beginnings, best experienced visually. The rise in temperature after the winter months gives plants a renewed vigour with new shoots, leaves and flowers blooming. The first day of spring is called Basant Panchami, an auspicious day for new beginnings. Goddess Saraswati, the Hindu goddess of knowledge, is also worshipped on this day.

A number of communities across India celebrate their new year in April with good food, family, and enthusiasm.

Holi: Festivities and food

Quite a few Indian festivals are linked to a change in season. Holi, for example, falls at the end of winter and the start of spring. It is connected to the spring equinox and wheat harvest in western India. This also explains why Holi is celebrated in all the states in the North and West with much fervour, and not so much in the East and South, which are more rice harvesting states.

There are some special foods and drinks associated with this festival of colours. Pooran poli is sweet roti that is made in the western states. A filling of jaggery and chana dal is stuffed inside a flour-based thin roti and cooked with ghee, all the three ingredients i.e. wheat, jaggery and dal being harvested at this time of the year.

Kanji vada (urad dal vadas dipped in a liquid fermented by mustard seeds) and dahi vadas (urad dal vadas in yoghurt) are not only refreshing but also prepare the gut with beneficial bacteria for the summer. Gujiya is the hallmark sweet made during Holi. It is a shortcrust kind of flour casing stuffed with reduced milk (khoya), nuts, coconut and dried fruits, prepared in half-moon shapes and deep-fried (sometimes even baked).

Holi is incomplete without thandai, a milk-based drink made using a mix of nuts (almonds, pistachios), watermelon seeds, poppy seeds and cooling ingredients like rose petals, fennel and cardamom, with an optional spike of bhaang (cannabis) to indulge in Holi merry making, free of all inhibitions. Some other favourites include sweets like malpua, ghewar, and coconut laddoos.

Spring time and Ayurveda

Ayurveda places a lot of importance on ritucharya* to keep the body attuned and immune through seasons and as a preventive measure against lifestyle disorders. Ritucharya comprises rules and regimens for diet and lifestyle to acclimatize the body to the seasons without altering body homeostasis.

As per Ayurveda, the months of mid-March to mid-May are considered as spring time. This helps prepare the body for the hottest months of the year, getting rid of the toxins accumulated from eating a lot of rich food in the winters.

Nourishing and rejuvenating practises help the body cope with the changing seasons, in tune with nature, also in a rejuvenation mode, during spring. Ayurveda recommends including spices like turmeric, cumin, coriander and fennel in food during this period to stimulate digestion and aid detoxification.

The flavour of the season is astringent. Food items tasting tikta (bitter), katu (pungent), and kashaya (astringent) are recommended. Avoiding heavy cold meals and sipping warm water through the day is also said to help during this time of the year. Recommended foods are wheat, barley, honey, green gram, red gram, tulsi, neem, turmeric, water boiled with ginger. Ritucharya also recommends avoiding daytime naps to reduce lethargy.

Pickling in springtime

Pickling is an age-old practice in India. The intent was to preserve the produce available in a narrow seasonal window and make it last all year. Salt and oil are the main ingredients that help preserve the vegetables/fruits being pickled. Moisture is a pickle's worst enemy. The end of spring to early summer is therefore the favoured time for pickling when the weather is dry and there is less humidity.

A number of basic pickle recipes involve careful selection of the ingredients, chopping it to specifications, mixing it with salt and turmeric, and allowing it to sundry. The marinated ingredient is then tossed in the oil of choice, either gingelly (in the South) or mustard (in the North and East), along with a mix of spices like red chilli powder, fenugreek seeds, mustard seeds, fennel, asafoetida in different combinations as per the region and the recipe being followed.

Mangoes are one of the favourite fruits to be pickled and nearly every region and community in India has its own recipe for a mango pickle. In Gujarati cuisine, Rajapuri varieties of mangoes that are large in size, firm and sour are used to make a sweet and spicy preserve, called *chundo*. A similar preparation, called *murabba,* is prepared in North India with crushed green cardamom and saffron. Saffron gives this preserve rich golden hues. Most Tamilians adore their *vadumanga*, a simple pickle of baby green mangoes in red chilli powder and mustard powder flavoured brine. *Avakkaya* is Andhra's gift to India. Made with whole garlic cloves or the addition of brown chickpeas, making this is an art unto itself.

Music to cook: Scan this QR Code to listen to India's spring raagas with a custom playlist.

SCAN ME

* Central Council for Research in Ayurvedic Sciences, Ministry of Ayush, Government of India. Available at http://www.ccras.nic.in/content/basant-ritucharya-spring-season-regimen

Appetizers, Drinks, Condiments

Aam Panna

Raw Mango Beverage

TIME TAKEN: 30 MINUTES | SERVES 4

A favourite thirst quencher for hot days made from raw mangoes, aam panna is regularly made in homes in north, west and eastern parts of India, each infused with local variations. Fire roasting the raw mangoes gives the drink a delicious smoky flavour.

Ingredients

1 large (350 g) raw mango
½ cup (80 g) raw cane sugar or
   powdered jaggery
½ cup water

FOR EACH GLASS
¼ tsp black salt
½ tsp roasted cumin powder
2-3 mint leaves for garnish

Method

1. Roast the raw mango directly over the stove flame, rotating periodically until the skin is completely charred. Once done, a knife should be able to pass through the flesh easily.
2. Peel off the skin and extract all the pulp into a mixer jar. To this, add the sugar and ½ cup water and blend to a puree.
3. Transfer to a saucepan over medium heat and bring to a simmer. The concentrate for the aam panna is ready. This can be kept in a sealed bottle in the refrigerator for upto one week.
4. To prepare the aam panna, in a glass, mix 1 part concentrate with 1 part water, 3-4 ice cubes, black salt, and roasted cumin powder. Garnish with mint leaves and serve.
5. You can also add green cardamom powder or saffron strands to the concentrate.

Thandai

Drink with Nuts and Spices – a Holi Speciality

TIME TAKEN: 20 MINUTES | MAKES AROUND 16 SERVINGS

Spices, nuts, and seeds are some of the ingredients that go into the making of this festive spicy-sweet beverage called thandai. Mixed with milk and sugar and served chilled, this welcome energizer is synonymous with the festival of Holi.

Ingredients

¼ cup (40 g) almonds
¼ cup (40 g) cashews
¼ cup (40 g) pistachios
¼ cup (35 g) melon seeds
3 tbsp fennel seeds
2 tbsp green cardamom pods
2 tsp black pepper
2 tbsp poppy seeds
2 tbsp dried rose petals

TO PREPARE 1 SERVING OF THANDAI
1 cup milk
1 tbsp sugar
Saffron strands and rose petals for garnish

Method

1. In a heavy-bottomed pan, on low to medium heat, toast the almonds, cashews, pistachios, melon seeds, fennel seeds, cardamom, and black pepper for 3-4 minutes.
2. Turn off the heat. Add the poppy seeds and dried rose petals. Combine with the rest of the ingredients. Leave to cool.
3. Once the ingredients cool, transfer to a blender and pulse 5-6 times to blend into a powder. Don't run the blender continuously or the oils will get extracted from the nuts and seeds. Your thandai mix is ready.
4. To make the drink, take 2 tablespoons of the thandai mix, 1 tablespoon of sugar, 4-5 ice cubes, and 1 cup milk in a blender. Blend for 30 seconds on high speed until the sugar and ice melt.
5. Transfer to a glass and garnish with rose petals and saffron strands. Serve chilled.

Panagam

A Sweet Spicy Beverage from South India

TIME TAKEN: 5 MINUTES | SERVES 4

Panagam is a drink prepared for the festival of Ram Navami, which is celebrated during spring time in South India. It is served along with kosumalli and neer moar (dilute spiced buttermilk). Ginger and cardamom are good digestives making this an ideal drink to be served at the end of a heavy meal. In his book, *Prohibition At Any Cost*, M.K. Gandhi writes, 'As a very good substitute for drink (alcoholic drinks), I suggest the ancient practice of drinking panagam be revived. It is made of cold water, jaggery, lime juice, and sabja seeds. This will give energy and also cool the system.'

Ingredients

3 cups (720 ml) water
½ cup (100 g) grated jaggery
1½ tsp ground ginger (sonth)
½ tsp green cardamom powder
2 tbsp lime juice

Method

1. Combine the grated jaggery along with the water in a bowl. Stir well until it is dissolved.
2. Add in the remaining ingredients. Stir to combine well. Serve chilled.

• If you cannot find dried ground ginger, grate 2-3 tablespoons of fresh ginger. Wrap it in a muslin cloth and squeeze out the juice.

Banana Raita

Ripe Bananas in Yoghurt

TIME TAKEN: 10 MINUTES | SERVES 4

When you have overripe bananas, give banana bread a break and try this raita instead. The sweet and creamy raita is the perfect foil for spicy rice dishes. It can also be had as a healthy dessert at the end of a meal. Be generous with the tempering, as the crunchy mustard seeds and urad dal offer a delicious texture to the dish.

Ingredients

1½ cups (400 g) yoghurt
½ tsp salt
2 medium sized (250 g) overripe bananas
1 tbsp peanut oil
1 tsp mustard seeds
2 tsp urad dal
2 dried red chillies, broken
1 sprig curry leaves

Method

1. In a bowl, whisk yoghurt and salt until there are no lumps.
2. Peel the bananas and crush them coarsely using a fork. Transfer the crushed bananas into the yoghurt bowl and combine well.
3. Heat the oil in a small tempering ladle.
4. Fry the mustard seeds, urad dal, chillies, and curry leaves. When the mustard seeds stop sputtering, gently pour the tempering over the banana-yoghurt mix.
5. Serve chilled or at room temperature with a spicy rice dish.

Kosumalli

Vegetable and Moong Dal Light Springtime Salad

PREP TIME: 30 MINUTES; COOKING TIME: 5 MINUTES; TIME TAKEN: 1 HOUR | SERVES 4-6

One of the popular Indian salads that is made on the occasion of the festival of Ram Navami. I have seen huge vats of this salad made in the streets of old Bengaluru on this day along with spiced buttermilk to be served to one and all. It is traditionally made with grated cucumber, but you can add other ingredients like raw mangoes, carrots, bell peppers, and so on.

Ingredients

- 2 medium sized (250 g) carrots
- 1 medium sized (120 g) cucumber
- 1 large (200 g) green capsicum
- ¼ cup (50 g) yellow moong dal
- 3 green chillies, sliced
- ¼ cup (20 g) fresh grated coconut
- ¼ cup chopped fresh coriander
- 1 tsp salt
- 1-2 limes, juiced
- 2 tsp oil
- ½ tsp mustard seeds
- ½ tsp cumin seeds

Method

1. Soak the moong dal in warm water for 30 minutes.
2. Peel and grate the carrots. Peel and grate the cucumber and keep it in a sieve for 10 minutes to drain the excess liquid. Grate the capsicum, discarding the seeds and the core.
3. Drain the moong dal, discarding the soaking water.
4. In a bowl, combine the grated vegetables along with the moong dal.
5. Add in the green chillies, fresh coconut, coriander, salt, and lime juice.
6. Heat the oil in a small tempering ladle. Fry mustard seeds and cumin seeds. Once the mustard seeds pop, transfer it over the salad.
7. Serve it chilled along with a glass of spiced thin buttermilk (chhaas).

- *Instead of split yellow moong dal, sprouts prepared from green moong beans can also be used, either raw or lightly steamed to make kosumalli.*
- *Shelled pomegranate is another much loved addition to this refreshing salad.*

Khamang Kakdi

Maharashtrian Cucumber Salad

TIME TAKEN: 30 MINUTES | SERVES 4

This cucumber salad from Maharashtra deserves a place among the most iconic salads of the world. Think of it as a chopped salad with cucumbers, but with the stamp of Indian food all over it, the spicy tadka, the gentle touch of fresh coconut, the bold flavours of coriander, and the crunch from the peanuts. Traditionally, a couple of spoons of this salad are served along with the rest of the dishes in the thali, but you can very well make a bowl of this for a snack or a light meal.

Ingredients

3 (400 g) medium-sized cucumbers
½ tsp salt
2 green chillies, finely chopped
¼ cup finely chopped fresh coriander
1 tbsp lime juice
2 tbsp fresh coconut
½ tsp ground cumin
½ tsp sugar
2 tsp peanut oil
1 green chilli, sliced
1 tsp cumin seeds
¼ cup roasted peanuts

Method

1. Peel and finely dice the cucumbers. Toss along with salt and place in a colander for 15 minutes to drain. Combine the cucumber with chopped chillies, coriander, lime juice, coconut, ground cumin, and sugar.

2. Heat oil in a small pan. Fry chillies and cumin seeds and transfer over the cucumber. Crush roasted peanuts coarsely and mix into the salad just before you serve.

Aam Ki Launji

A Sweet, Sour, and Spicy Raw Mango Chutney

TIME TAKEN: 25 MINUTES | MAKES AROUND 2 CUPS

The appearance of raw mangoes in markets means its pickling season. There's a staggering variety of pickles in India and raw mangoes are one of the most popular ingredients to make pickles. Pickle making is a very precise process, from choosing the ingredients to precautions while making the pickle, allowing it to mature and storing it safely. However, there are easier recipes, such as aam ki launji that can perk up a simple meal.

Ingredients

2 medium sized (350 g) raw mangoes
2 tbsp mustard oil*
1 tsp mustard seeds
1 tsp cumin seeds
1 tsp fennel seeds
1 tsp nigella seeds
½ tsp carom seeds
$1/8$ tsp asafoetida**
½ tsp salt
½ cup (80 g) crushed jaggery
½ tsp ground turmeric
2 tsp Kashmiri red chilli powder
1 tsp black salt

Method

1. Peel and chop the raw mangoes into 1-2" long pieces around 1 cm thick. Don't cut it too thin as the launji should still have intact pieces of the raw mango once it is ready.
2. In a pan, heat the mustard oil. Once it is smoking and turns a shade lighter, add the mustard seeds. Once it stops sputtering, add the cumin seeds, fennel seeds, nigella seeds, and carom seeds. Fry for 20-30 seconds.
3. Stir in the asafoetida, followed by the chopped raw mango. Toss on a medium heat to coat well with spices. Season with half teaspoon of salt. Pour in a cup and a quarter of water. Bring this to a boil over high heat. Reduce the heat to low, cover and cook for another 6-8 minutes until the mango pieces are tender. The time taken will depend on the variety and the size of the pieces, so keep a watch. Don't let it overcook.
4. Crumble in the jaggery at this point. Sprinkle turmeric, chilli powder, and black salt. Stir and allow to cook over high heat until the jaggery melts. Simmer this for 3-4 minutes until the sauce thickens a bit. Don't simmer for too long as it will continue to thicken on cooling.
5. Remove to a clean dry glass bottle when cool and store in the fridge. Use within a month.

* *Mustard oil adds great flavour to this condiment. If you don't have it, any other vegetable oil can be used.*

** *Increase asafoetida to ½ teaspoon if using compound variety that is not as strong as the pure form.*

Main Course

Vegetarian Parsi Dhansak

Parsi Style Lentils with Vegetables

COOKING TIME: 45 MINUTES | SERVES 6

Dhansak is a meat and lentil dish prepared by the Parsi community. The term dhansak comes from combining the words dhan and saak, which mean dal and vegetables respectively. Although the traditional dish includes meat, this vegetarian version is a hearty dish with plenty of seasonal vegetables and greens and an intense flavour from the special spice mix (dhansak masala).

Ingredients

$1/3$ cup (65 g) split pigeon peas (tur dal)
$2/3$ cup (130 g) split pink lentils (masoor dal)
400 grams yellow pumpkin
1 small bunch (30 g) spring onion greens
2 cups (100 g) fenugreek leaves
2 small (50 g) brinjals
½ tsp ground turmeric
6 cloves garlic
1½ inches ginger root, sliced
1-2 tbsp ghee
2 medium sized onions, finely chopped
4 medium sized tomatoes, chopped
2 tbsp dhansak masala* (see pg 23)
1½ tsp salt

Method

1. Wash the lentils well. Transfer to a pressure cooker with 3 cups of water. Pressure cook over high heat until full pressure (1 whistle) is reached. Reduce the heat to low and cook for 15 minutes. Once the pressure subsides, open the cooker, mash the lentils with a ladle, and keep aside.

2. While the lentils are cooking, peel, deseed, and chop the pumpkin into large chunks. Slice the stem end of the eggplant and chop into quarters. Slice the spring onions (only greens) into batons. Finely chop the fenugreek leaves. Place all the above in a pressure cooker with 1 cup water, pinch of turmeric and salt. Cook for 1 whistle.

3. Peel garlic cloves and crush to a coarse paste along with sliced ginger and a pinch of salt.

4. Heat the ghee in a heavy-bottomed pan. Add the freshly prepared ginger-garlic paste and chopped onions. Sauté over medium heat for 5-6 minutes.

5. Add the chopped tomatoes, ½ tsp salt and stir continuously over high heat, until the tomatoes turn pulpy.

6. Add the dhansak masala (readymade or see page 29 for recipe), and stir well until it is incorporated into the onion-tomato base, for around 3-4 minutes.

7. Now add the mashed lentils, coarsely mashed cooked vegetables, ½ cup water and bring to a simmer. Dhansak has a thick consistency, so add water cautiously. Taste and add up to ½ tsp salt, or as required. Simmer for 4-5 minutes over low heat.

8. Traditionally, dhansak is served as a smooth puree. So, once cooled, you can blend this into a puree and reheat when ready to serve.

9. Serve hot with steamed rice and kachumber (Parsi-style onion-tomato-cucumber salad) on the side.

Kheere Ki Subzi

Rajasthani Cucumber Curry

COOKING TIME: 20 MINUTES | SERVES 6

Cucumbers are commonly used in salads and not so much in curries. Combining them with onions, tomatoes and a mix of spice powders makes a quick vegetable side dish that goes well with rotis. A touch of besan or mashed chana dal can be added to thicken the sauce.

Ingredients

7-8 (800 g) European cucumbers
2 tbsp mustard oil
1 tsp cumin seeds
1 sprig curry leaves
2 green chillies, sliced
1 tbsp chopped garlic
1 small onion, chopped
1 medium sized tomato, chopped
2 tsp ground coriander
1 tsp red chilli powder
1 tsp raw mango powder (amchoor)
1½ tsp salt
2 tbsp chopped fresh coriander leaves

Method

1. Slice off the top and bottom of the cucumbers and cut into a medium dice (~2 cm).
2. Heat the oil in a pan. Fry cumin seeds for a few seconds. Add the curry leaves, chillies, garlic, and onions. Fry over medium heat for 3-4 minutes.
3. Stir in chopped tomatoes and fry for another 2-3 minutes.
4. Add the chopped cucumber along with the spice powders and salt.
5. Toss well to combine and continue cooking over medium heat for 4-5 minutes so that the cucumbers are partially cooked but are retaining a bite.
6. Garnish with fresh coriander and serve with rotis or rice.

Thotakoora Vepudu

Amaranth Greens, Andhra Style

COOKING TIME: 20 MINUTES | SERVES 4-6

Indian cuisine uses a variety of local greens over and above spinach for everyday dishes. Every region has their own preferred local greens, either bought, grown at home or foraged. Amaranth greens, both the red and green variants, are used regularly in South Indian cuisine. This recipe is for a simple stir fry using green amaranth leaves that has a burst of flavour from garlic and the finishing layer of crushed roasted sesame seeds. Spinach makes an easy substitute in case these greens are not available.

Ingredients

2 tbsp (15 g) white sesame seeds
1 tbsp peanut oil
1 tsp black mustard seeds
1 sprig curry leaves
2 tsp Bengal gram (chana dal)
1 tsp urad dal
2 dried red chillies, broken into pieces
2 green chillies, slit
4 cloves garlic, peeled and crushed
1 large onion, peeled and diced
6-7 cups (350 g) of chopped green
    amaranth leaves*
½ tsp salt
½ tsp ground turmeric

Method

1. In a pan over medium heat, toast the sesame seeds for 4-5 minutes until they start popping. Remove to a dish and grind to a coarse powder when cool.
2. In the same pan, heat the oil.
3. Fry mustard seeds, curry leaves, chana dal, urad dal, and chillies until the seeds sputter and the dals turn a shade darker.
4. Add the garlic and onion. Sauté over medium heat for 4-5 minutes until onion is softened.
5. Stir in the chopped amaranth leaves. Turn the heat to high and sauté for 4-5 minutes.
6. Reduce the heat to medium, and add salt and ground turmeric. Mix well and cook for another 4-5 minutes.
7. Top with sesame powder, stir once to combine and serve with rice and dal.

* This is half a kilo of green amaranth that gives around 350 g of leaves. You may use tender stems, but discard the woody stems.

Tendli Bibbe Upkari

Konkani Ivy Gourd and Cashew Stir Fry

TIME TAKEN: 45 MINUTES I SERVES 4

This dry curry made using ivy gourd is a specialty of coastal Karnataka, the region of Mangalore. Cashew nuts plantations are very common in this part of the country. Tender cashews with skins are traditionally used in this dish. The skins are peeled off after soaking in hot water. As tender cashews are tough to procure in other parts of the world, the recipe below uses regular cashew nuts soaked in hot water to make it somewhat softer.

Ingredients

400 g ivy gourd (kundru)
$1/3$ cup (50 g) cashew nut halves
1 tbsp coconut oil
½ tsp black mustard seeds
2 tsp urad dal
2-3 dried red chillies, broken into pieces
Pinch of asafoetida
1 tsp salt
1 tsp crushed jaggery or brown sugar
2 tbsp fresh coconut

Method

1. Slice the two ends of the ivy gourd. Cut lengthwise into quarters to get around 2 heaped cups of chopped vegetables.
2. Soak the cashew nut halves in hot water for 30 minutes. Drain well and keep aside.
3. Heat oil in a pan. Fry mustard seeds for a few seconds. Once the sputtering stops, add urad dal and red chillies. Fry until urad dal turns light brown in colour. Stir in asafoetida.
4. Add the chopped ivy gourd and combine over high heat for 30 seconds.
5. Add around ¼ cup water to the pan. Cover and steam cook for 10 minutes or so until the gourd is tender.
6. Combine the cashews, salt, and jaggery. Stir to combine well.
7. Garnish with fresh coconut and serve hot with dal and rice.

- *Some of the ivy gourds may be red inside due to over ripening. While it is perfectly safe to eat these, they might be tougher, thereby taking longer to cook, and also not as flavourful as the tender ones. If you get a chance to pick and buy these, select smaller sized ones.*
- *If you cannot find ivy gourd, try this recipe using gherkins or baby zucchinis.*

Parval Subzi

Stuffed Pointed Gourd

TIME TAKEN: 40 MINUTES | SERVES 4-6

Parval is a common springtime and summer vegetable in the eastern parts of India. A lot of recipes featuring parval, or potol as it is called in Bengali, are a part of the Bengali cuisine. This recipe for stuffed parval, in which the gourds are stuffed with a freshly prepared spice paste, is from eastern parts of Uttar Pradesh. While gourds are a plentiful and inexpensive vegetable in India, slightly elaborate preparations like this one make a simple meal like dal and rice a little more special.

Ingredients

12 pieces (400 g) pointed gourd (parval)
½ tsp fenugreek seeds
2 tbsp coriander seeds
1 tsp fennel seeds
1 tsp dried mango powder
3 green chillies
6-8 cloves garlic
1 small onion, coarsely grated
½ tsp ground turmeric
1 tsp salt
2-3 tbsp chopped fresh coriander
3-4 tbsp mustard oil

Method

1. In a small pan over medium heat, dry roast the fenugreek seeds, coriander seeds, and fennel seeds by stirring continuously. Once the seeds are aromatic and a shade darker, remove to a dish and cool. Grind to a powder and keep aside. You can add the dry mango powder at this stage.

2. Crush or grind the green chillies and garlic to a coarse paste and add to the prepared spice powder.

3. To the above mix, add the grated onion, turmeric, salt, and chopped coriander. Add 2 teaspoons of mustard oil to this and mix well.

4. Wash and slice off the two ends of the pointed gourd. Using a paring knife, make a slit lengthwise. Pry it open a bit and fill a teaspoon of the prepared masala into the gourd. There's no need to remove the inner membranes and seeds. Similarly, slit and stuff all the gourds. Keep any remaining masala aside.

5. Heat all of the remaining oil.

6. Place the gourds carefully in a single layer on the oil. Cover and cook over medium heat for 5 minutes. Open the lid and turn them over to cook the other side. Cover and cook for another 5-7 minutes. At this point, add any of the leftover masala to the pan. Gently stir it together with the gourd. Allow this to cook in an open pan for another 5-7 minutes until the gourds are cooked through.

7. Serve hot with dal–rice or with rotis.

• *Thickly sliced potatoes can be added along with the gourd while cooking. Wedges of potato can be slit and stuffed with the masala and cooked similarly. You can also try a similar recipe using baby eggplants.*

Vatha Kuzhambu

A Tamarind-based Saucy Side Dish

TIME TAKEN: 30 MINUTES | SERVES 4-6

The very mention of vatha kuzhambu can induce homesickness in Tamil folks away from home. The tangy, hot, and mildly sweet liquid served with hot rice and gingelly (South Indian sesame oil) is a must try!

Ingredients

4 tbsp (30 g) tamarind flakes

FOR SPICE PASTE
1 tsp gingelly oil
5 dried red chillies
2 sprig curry leaves
2 tbsp dehusked and split black gram (urad dal)
2 tbsp split pigeon peas (tur dal)
1 tsp black peppercorns
¼ tsp fenugreek seeds
----
3 tbsp gingelly oil
2 tbsp dried turkey berries or nightshade berries (sundakka or manathakkalika)
1 tsp mustard seeds
¼ tsp fenugreek seeds
½ tsp cumin seeds
1 sprig curry leaves
1½ tsp salt
1 tsp crushed jaggery

Method

1. Soak the tamarind flakes in 2 cups of hot water in a bowl. Keep aside for 15-20 minutes. Squeeze the tamarind with your fingers to extract all the pulp into the water. Discard the pith and the seeds. Keep this extract on the side.
2. To prepare the fresh spice paste, in a heavy-bottomed pan, heat 1 teaspoon oil. Add all the ingredients for the spice paste and sauté over medium heat for 4-5 minutes until the dals turn golden in colour. Remove and cool for 10 minutes. Transfer to a mixer jar and grind to a fine paste using around half cup of water. Keep aside.
3. In the same pan, heat 3 tablespoons of oil. Fry the dried turkey berries for 30 seconds to a minute until they turn a few shades darker and crisp. Drain using a slotted spoon and remove to a bowl.
4. To the pan with the remaining oil, add the mustard seeds, fenugreek seeds, cumin seeds and curry leaves. Add the prepared tamarind extract to the pan along with the salt. Bring this to a boil and then simmer for 6-7 minutes. This is to thicken the tamarind water and also cook the raw smell of the tamarind.
5. Add the freshly ground spice paste to the reduced tamarind extract. Use half cup of water to rinse the mixer jar and add to the pan. Stir well, add the jaggery, and simmer the sauce for 5-7 minutes.
6. Turn off the heat and add the fried turkey berries. Serve with hot rice and gingelly oil or ghee.

Kodamilagai Sadham

Capsicum Rice

TIME TAKEN: 45 MINUTES | SERVES 6

Capsicum rice is made in Tamil as well as Kannada cuisine. This recipe has flavours from both states.

Ingredients

2 large (450 g) capsicums, deseeded, chopped into bite sized pieces
1½ cups (300 g) rice (short grain, aromatic, like Seeraga samba)
2 tbsp peanut oil
2 bay leaves
1 stick cinnamon
4 cloves
1 tsp mustard seeds
1 tbsp Bengal gram (chana dal)
1 tbsp dehusked and split black gram (urad dal)
2-3 dried red chillies
¼ cup (40 g) peanuts
2 tsp salt
1-2 tbsp gingelly oil

FOR SPICE MIX
½ tsp coconut oil
4 dried red chillies
2 tbsp Bengal gram (chana dal)
1 tbsp dehusked and split black gram (urad dal)
3 tbsp coriander seeds
1 tsp cumin seeds
½ tsp black peppercorns
3 1" long cinnamon sticks
5-6 cloves
3 green cardamoms
2 bay leaves
2 tbsp sesame seeds
¼ cup desiccated coconut
1 tbsp jaggery (optional)
1 tbsp tamarind flakes

Method

1. Cook rice with 3 cups of water, (see page 23). Fluff with a fork and keep aside.
2. In a large pan, heat one tablespoon of oil over low-medium heat. Fry bay leaves, cinnamon, cloves, mustard seeds, chana dal, urad dal, and dried red chillies until the dals turn golden brown. Add the peanuts. Fry for 2-3 minutes or until they turn crisp. Add the diced capsicum and stir fry for 6-7 minutes until the capsicum is cooked. Set aside.
3. Meanwhile, prepare the spice mix. Heat ½ teaspoon oil in a wok over low heat. Add the spices (red chilli through bay leaves). Toast until the dals are lightly golden and the mix is aromatic (around 7 minutes). Remove and cool. In the same wok, lightly toast the coconut until fragrant (around 2 minutes). Remove from the wok and set aside in a bowl. Next, toast the sesame seeds in the wok until they pop (around 2 minutes). Remove and cool.
4. In a mixer, pulse the above spice mix along with the soaked tamarind and jaggery, until you get a coarse moist powder.
5. To assemble, place capsicum-peanut mix in a large pan over low heat, add the rice and spice mix. Season with salt and mix over for 3-4 minutes. Add 1-2 tablespoons of gingelly oil for a final layer of flavour. Combine well and transfer to a serving dish.

Achinga Payru Thoran

Long Beans Stir Fry

Thoran is prepared with a variety of vegetables such as cabbage, greens, beans, carrot, snake gourd, ivy gourd, etc. Long beans, with their unique flavour, are one of the favourite vegetables to prepare thoran in Kerala cuisine. It is served as a part of the Onam sadhya (a traditional banana leaf meal).

Ingredients

250 g long beans, chopped
½ tsp salt
½ tsp sugar
1 tbsp coconut oil
½ tsp mustard seeds
2 tsp urad dal
1 sprig curry leaves
2 dried red chillies
2-3 green chillies chopped
2-3 tbsp freshly grated coconut (or frozen)
Salt, to taste

Method

1. Steam the chopped beans in a pressure cooker along with ½ cup water, ½ tsp salt, and ½ tsp sugar. After one whistle, turn off the flame and open the cooker by releasing the steam. This retains the green colour and prevents overcooking. Drain by passing through a sieve.*
2. Green beans can also be cooked in the microwave (4-5 minutes) or by boiling in a pan on stove top.
3. In a pan, heat coconut oil. Fry the mustard seeds and when it stops popping, add urad dal, curry leaves, and chillies.
4. To this, add the cooked beans.
5. Adjust for salt and add coconut. Toss to combine. Serve hot with rice and dal.

The drained water can be used in soups/dals.

Khatte Meethe Kaddu

Sour and Sweet Pumpkin

COOKING TIME: 15 MINUTES | SERVES 4

This sweet sour and spicy pumpkin dish is a rustic dry curry prepared in many communities in North India. It is also called 'halwai' (sweetshop)-style or bhandare wale kaddu. As it has no onion or garlic, it is considered suitable to be served as an offering in worship.

Ingredients

400 grams orange pumpkin, peeled and cubed
1 tbsp mustard oil
Pinch of asafoetida
½ tsp mustard seeds
¼ tsp fenugreek seeds
½ tsp cumin seeds
2 tsp dried mango powder (amchoor)
1 tsp red chilli powder
2 tsp ground coriander
¼ tsp ground turmeric
½ tsp garam masala powder
1 tbsp crushed jaggery
1 tsp salt
1 tbsp chopped fresh coriander for garnish

Method

1. Heat the oil in a heavy-bottomed pan. Add the asafoetida, mustard seeds, fenugreek seeds, and cumin seeds. Once the mustard seeds splutters, add the pumpkin cubes and toss well, to coat with oil and whole spices. Sauté for 2-3 minutes.
2. Add all the remaining ground spices and give it a stir.
3. Sprinkle crushed jaggery and add ½ cup of water. Cover and cook over low heat. This will take around 10 minutes to cook. Give it a stir intermittently and sprinkle some water if it's sticking to the bottom of the pan.
4. The pumpkin is done when you can pass a fork through it. The final dish should have a balance of spicy, sweet, and sour.
5. Garnish with fresh coriander. Serve with hot puris.

Shengdanyachi Amti

Peanut Curry

COOKING TIME: 20 MINUTES | SERVES 6

This dal-like dish made using peanuts is unique to Maharashtrian fasting dishes when the usual grains and legumes are abstained from. This richly flavoured sauce is usually served along with vari or bhagar, which is cooked barnyard millet grains. The amti can also be served with plain rice.

Ingredients

1 cup (150 g) peanuts
2 green chillies
2 pieces kokum
1 tsp salt
2 tsp jaggery or sugar
1 tbsp chopped fresh coriander

TEMPERING
2 tsp ghee
1 tsp cumin seeds
2 slit green chillies
2-3 cloves (optional)

Method

1. In a pan roast the peanuts over low to medium heat for 8-10 minutes until well roasted. Don't let them brown as it will impart a bitter taste to the dish. Remove to a dish and cool.
2. Place the roasted peanuts in a mixer jar and, using the pulse function, crush it to a fine powder. Take care not to run the mixer continuously and for too long or it will turn into peanut butter.
3. In a heavy-bottomed pan over medium heat, combine the peanut powder with 3 cups of water. Season with salt and sugar. Add the kokum pieces to this mixture. Bring to a boil. Reduce the heat and simmer for 8-10 minutes while stirring every now and then.
4. To prepare the tempering, heat the ghee in a small tempering ladle or pan. Add cumin seeds, green chillies, and cloves and fry for a few seconds. Transfer it over the amti and garnish with coriander leaves. Pair it with vari cha chawal (page 140).

Sweets

Gujiya

Deep Fried Sweet Dumplings

TIME TAKEN: 1½ HOURS | MAKES 24

These are a Holi specialty in North India, a signature sweet of springtime. It goes by different names in many parts of India - ghughra (Gujarat), somasi (Tamil), karani (Marathi), and kajjkaya (Telugu). Apparently, this preparation dates back to the thirteenth century, in which a jaggery and honey mixture was coated with wheat flour and sun dried.

Ingredients

2 cups (200 g) all-purpose flour
4 tbsp ghee (soft)

FOR FILLING
2 tsp ghee
2 tbsp fine semolina (chiroti rava)
3 tbsp desiccated coconut
2 tbsp cashew halves
12 almonds
2 tbsp raisins
½ cup (100 g) solidified milk (khoya)
½ cup (100 g) sugar (coarsely powdered
   in mixer)
½ tsp green cardamom powder
2 cups ghee or neutral flavoured
   oil for deep-frying

Method

1. Take the flour in a large bowl. Add the ghee to the flour and rub with fingertips until it is well absorbed into the flour and you get the consistency of wet sand. When clumped together, the flour should hold its shape. If not, add a little more ghee and rub it into the dough. To this, add lukewarm water by the tablespoon (roughly a total of 80-90 ml) to make a medium stiff dough. Knead until it is smooth. Keep covered with a damp cotton towel for 30 minutes.

2. Meanwhile, prepare the filling for the gujiya.

3. Heat 2 tsp ghee in a pan. Sauté the rava over low to medium heat for 2-3 minutes. Add the desiccated coconut to the rava and sauté for another minute. Remove this into a plate.

4. Chop the cashews and almonds to small bits. Toast these in the pan over medium heat for 1-2 minutes. Add it to the rava-coconut mix.

5. Chop the raisins coarsely and combine with the above mixture.

6. In the hot pan, crumble the khoya and sauté over a medium flame for 5-6 minutes until it turns somewhat golden in colour. Transfer it to the plate with all the other ingredients.

7. Lastly, mix in the sugar and cardamom powder.
8. It is easy to shape the gujiyas if you have a special mould. Divide the dough into 18-20 gram portions. Roll into balls. Roll out each ball into a thin circle, around 4 inches in diameter. Place the circle over the open mould. Moisten the circumference using a finger dipped in water. Place 1-2 teaspoons of the filling in the lower half of the circle. Close the mould shut tightly so the edges get crimped and sealed. Remove the excess dough outside of the mould.
9. If you don't have a mould, roll out each ball into a 4" circle. Moisten the circumference using a finger dipped in water. Place the filling into the lower half of the circle. Fold the upper half over the lower half to make a semicircle. Press the edges down to seal. The edges can be crimped using the tines of a fork or folded over all around.
10. Using this method, prepare all the gujiyas and keep them under a moist cotton towel at all times to prevent drying out.
11. Heat ghee or oil in a pan. When the ghee is medium hot, put in the gujiyas 3-4 at a time (depending on the size of the pan) and allow to fry over medium-low heat for a total of 15 minutes so that the entire casing is cooked, golden on the outside and crisped up. The next batches may take slightly less time.

- *Turn them over only after 5-7 minutes to prevent splitting open.*
- *Handle the gujiyas very gently right from dropping them into the oil and throughout the frying process.*
- *Poking very tiny holes in the gujiya before frying using a toothpick also prevents them from splitting open. Do not overstuff the gujiyas.*

Chikki

Peanut Brittle

TIME TAKEN: 40 MINUTES | MAKES 12-14 PIECES

In the Indian joint families, laddoo making was a family activity. The women of the house would finish their daily chores and the clean up after lunch, sit down on the kitchen floor and get down to making laddoos or other sweets and savouries for tea times. Stories and family gossip would be shared and quick work would be made of labour intensive cooking. These ground-nut laddoos are not laborious to make, but they don't lack in deliciousness.

Ingredients

1 cup (150 g) peanuts
1 cup (150 g) powdered jaggery
1 tsp ghee

Method

1. In a heavy-bottomed pan over medium heat, roast the peanuts for 8-10 minutes with constant stirring. It should be crisp when you bite into it on cooling.
2. Remove to a deep dish and crush with hands to loosen skins. Blow on the peels to discard them (over a sink). Keep the roasted skinned peanuts aside.
3. If you get readymade roasted skinned unsalted peanuts, use them. But do toast it for a few minutes to make it crisp before using.
4. In a pan over medium heat, take the jaggery with ¼ cup water. Allow this to come to a boil. Reduce the heat and let it simmer for another 5-6 minutes. Keep a bowl of cold water handy to check the consistency of the syrup. Pour ½ tsp worth of syrup in the water and roll it into a long rope with finger tips. Initially it will roll into a soft ball. We are looking for the next stage of syrup. If this rope breaks with a crunch then it is ready for use. You can also roll this syrup poured in the water into a ball and if it falls with a sharp sound indicating hardness, then the syrup is ready.
5. Turn off the heat and add the peanuts. Mix well, and, once slightly cooled, roll into balls between greased palms. You can also grease a tray and press the mixture into the tray, smoothing the top with a greased spatula. Cut into pieces when still warm and break along the cuts. Store in an airtight container.

- *The time taken can be cut down if you use unsalted roasted skinned peanuts.*
- *The same recipe can be tried with a mix of nuts, crushed coarsely, along with some toasted sesame seeds.*

Chak Hao

Manipuri Black Rice Kheer

PREP TIME: 12 HOURS; COOKING TIME: 1 HOUR 15 MINUTES | SERVES 6

This kheer recipe is from the state of Manipur in Northeast India, using the local Manipuri black rice. Soaking the rice for 12 hours is mandatory so that it cooks to a creamy texture. The stunning lilac colour of this dessert along with the aroma of coconut milk makes all the wait worth it.

Ingredients

¼ cup (40-50 g) black rice
1 litre whole cream milk
½ cup (100 g) sugar
2 tbsp milk powder
½ cup (120 g) thick coconut milk

FOR GARNISH
Thinly sliced fresh coconut
Dried rose petals

Method

1. Wash the rice and soak for 12 hours in water 1 inch above the level of rice.
2. Take the soaked rice along with the water and milk and cook it either on stove top with constant stirring or an electronic pressure cooker (pressure cook setting, high pressure, 1 hour). Once the pressure lowers, open the cooker. The rice should be fully cooked and sticky at this point. The milk will be light purple in colour due to the colour of the rice and the soaking water added at the cooking stage.
3. Add the sugar and stir well over low heat. You can either pressure cook for another 10 minutes at this stage or allow it to simmer for 10 minutes.
4. In a small bowl, whisk the milk powder and coconut milk. Add it to the kheer and simmer for another 5 minutes over low heat. Add thinly sliced coconut to the kheer.
5. Garnish with dried rose petals. Serve chilled.

summer

Unlike Europe, which comes alive in summer, Indian summers are harsher, at least in the plains. The season is a waiting room we enter after spring and bide our time until winter. The weather is all heat and dust, and with worse luck, soul-sapping humidity.

Summers in India swing between the extremely hot to moderate to rather cool depending on the altitude. Hill stations like Shimla, Mussourie, Dalhousie, Munnar, Ooty, and Mahabaleshwar remain much cooler than the plains. The officers of the British Raj, unable to bear the summers in India, would escape to these places.

In India's coastal cities, for instance in Mumbai, the summer months are uncomfortably humid. I remember that the school summer holidays kept us home for two whole months. Days were slow with a constant hum of boredom that led to many silly creative pursuits. It was too hot to sleep off the afternoons or to be playing outdoors. Finding a cold nimbu sharbat or one of the coloured synthetic concentrates in the fridge was like striking upon a gold mine.

However, life does not slow down like this for the farmers even in places where the temperatures rise enough to give people a sun-stroke. They are busy preparing the soil for monsoons. Summer ploughing helps expose the soil to the sun, killing any larvae and eggs hiding under the soil surface. It also uproots weeds and reduces the incidence of soil-borne diseases, pests, and weeds. Leaf manure and cow dung manure is added to the soil to improve its fertility for the next cropping cycle. In between, the rabi and kharif crops, short cycle crops including seasonal vegetables are grown.

Mangoes and Indian summers

The Indian mango season is a festival unto itself. Fossil evidence has shown that mangoes made their first appearance in the Northeast along with Myanmar and Bangladesh around 25 to 30 million years ago. It is no surprise then that mango is integral to our culture and is the national fruit of India.

Online wars are fought over which mango variety is the best, judging its size, aroma, sweetness, and price, among other things. There are the Alphonso fans and those who prefer other regional varieties. Mangoes are harvested at different periods in different areas through the year depending on geography, variety, and climate. Varieties like Amrapali, Mallika, Langra and Himsagar are harvested in the northeastern regions of India between the months of May and June.

Most Gujarati households don't go a day without aamras during season, served as a part of the lunch thali, along with dal, rice, vegetable and roti or puri. Fajeto is a buttermilk-based zero-waste curry made with the pulp stuck to the stone and peels, after aamras is extracted from these mangoes. In Kerala cuisine, baby-sized ripe mangoes are used in a yoghurt and coconut based pulisheri. In Maharastrian cuisine, mango pulp is added to the basic shrikhand recipe to get aamrakhand. Aam papad is one of the ways to preserve mango for months. Reduced fruit pulp is dried out on sheets and subsequently, rolled and preserved.

Traditional sweets like kheer, phirni, kulfi, burfi and peda are *mangofied* with abandon when the king of fruits is in season.

Gourd season

Gourds come into season at the end of spring. They are rich in water, easy on the stomach, and summer-friendly. Over fifteen varieties of vegetables belonging to the Cucurbita family are grown and consumed in the northeastern regions. Different varieties of pumpkin, wild cucumbers, bottle gourds, ridge gourds and sponge gourds are cultivated in the Northeast in both tropical and subtropical conditions. Tinda (apple gourd), nenua (sponge gourd), and lauki (bottle gourd) are the favoured gourds in the northern states. In West Bengal, parval or pointed gourd is a delicacy cooked in various styles. In Southern India, gourds are either added to sambar, or lightly steamed and topped with a tempering and fresh coconut or made into chutneys in combination with peanuts, coconut, and spices. Somehow, these mild-mannered vegetables don't seem to find favour with the present generations as they did with our parents and grandparents.

Sundried foods

We Indians are a resourceful lot and economize on all fronts, including with the sun. Harsh summer sun is harnessed to make homemade sundried goodies, which is stored through year, deep fried and served alongside a simple meal. Called *vethal* or *vadam* in Tamil, these crispies are made using a variety of recipes, many of them making use of rice flour, cooked rice, poha, sago, millets, ground lentils, chillies, onions, garlic etc. in varying combinations. Summer-produce like cluster beans, lady's fingers, turkey berries and chillies are also sundried after marinating them in salted buttermilk. These are used in the preparation of dishes like vatthakuzhambu.

Summer coolers

Cooling beverages make summers more bearable in India. And by cooling, I don't mean just iced cold, but also cooling herbs and spices like fennel, mint, bael (wood apple), rhododendron, sandalwood, sarsaparilla, vetiver, and ingredients like ragi, buttermilk, yoghurt that Ayurveda considers as cooling to the constitution of the body.

Panagam is a jaggery sweetened drink specially prepared and served on the festival of Ram Navami in the South. Neer mor or chaas, call it by any name but diluted buttermilk with the tempering of mustard seeds and curry leaves in the South or a sprinkling of roasted cumin powder and black salt in the North is an absolute thirst quencher.

In Bihar and UP, sattu is mixed into a glass of buttermilk for a filling as well as cooling drink.

In Karnataka, ragi flour is cooked and the paste is added to buttermilk along with spices. Called ragi ambli, this is hearty enough to make for a light breakfast.

Fennel seeds sherbet called variyali nu sharbat in Gujarati is a summer favourite featuring the cooling spice, raisins, rock salt, and sugar.

Rajasthan experiences a fiercely hot summer. A popular cooler in these parts is bajre ki raab or rabadi in which a paste of bajra flour and water is cooked and added to thinned yoghurt or buttermilk and flavoured with carom and cumin seeds, seasoned with salt.

Aam panna is a refreshing drink made using raw mangoes which are either charred on an open flame or cooked until soft and the pulp mixed with a sweetener and spiced

Cooking in the morning? Try out a custom morning raagas playlist. Scan QR Code to listen.

SCAN ME

Appetizers, Drinks, Condiments

Peerkangai Thogayal

Ridge Gourd Chutney

TIME TAKEN: 15 MINUTES | SERVES 4

The spiciness from the red chillies, the tanginess from the tamarind, and the pungency from asafoetida combine with the mildly flavoured ridge gourd, making it a delight to eat with hot rice and ghee.

Ingredients

2 medium-sized (400 g) ridge gourds (turai)
2 tsp gingelly oil
½ tsp black mustard seeds
3 dried red chillies
2 tbsp dehusked and split black gram (urad dal)
Pinch of asafoetida
½ cup (40 g) fresh grated coconut
1" piece of tamarind
½ tsp salt

TEMPERING
2 tsp gingelly oil
½ tsp black mustard seeds
1 tsp dehusked and split black gram (urad dal)
1 dried red chilli
1 sprig curry leaves

Method

1. Slice off the two ends of the ridge gourd. Lightly peel the ridges and slice.
2. Heat 1 teaspoon of oil in a pan and sauté the gourd slices for 4-5 minutes over high heat. Remove this to a dish to cool.
3. In the same pan, heat another teaspoon of oil. Add the mustard seeds, red chillies, urad dal, and asafoetida. Fry over medium heat until the dal turns golden.
4. In a mixer jar, take the sautéed ridge gourd slices, the fried spice-dal mix, coconut, tamarind, and salt and grind to a fine paste. Remove to a bowl.
5. To prepare the tempering, heat the oil and add mustard seeds, urad dal, red chilli, and curry leaves. Fry until the dal is golden. Transfer this over the thogayal.
6. Serve this with hot rice and ghee.

Murungakka Soup

Drumstick Soup

Both drumstick pods and leaves are made into a number of dishes in the South and the state of Odisha. Drumstick or moringa pods have a unique strong flavour and is a common vegetable added to sambar (see page 28). The flavour is showcased even better in this soup recipe that is adapted from Chettinad cuisine. The spice levels are kept to a minimum using just freshly crushed black pepper.

Ingredients

4 drumsticks
3 cloves garlic, sliced
1 medium sized onion, sliced
1 medium sized tomato, roughly chopped
1 tsp salt
¼ tsp ground turmeric
½ tsp crushed black pepper

GARNISH
Few mint leaves

Method

1. Wash and chop the drumsticks into 2-3" long pieces.
2. Take 2 cups water in a pressure cooker. To this, add the drumstick pieces, sliced garlic, onion, and tomato. Season with salt and turmeric. Close the lid and place the weight on. Pressure cook for one whistle (or until the cooker reaches full pressure). Remove from the heat and allow to cool.
3. Open the cooker, and fish out the drumstick pieces. Open out the drumstick pieces and using the edge of a teaspoon scrape out all the cooked flesh into a bowl.
4. Take this in a blender along with the remaining contents in the pressure cooker. Add the cooking liquids and blend to a smooth puree.
5. Transfer this to the cooker or a saucepan and bring to a simmer, thinning down with water as per the desired consistency. Season with freshly crushed black pepper in the end.
6. Divide between 4 small bowls. Garnish with a couple of mint leaves and serve hot.

• This can also be had as a rasam along with rice. Excess water from cooking dal can be used as the stock in this soup.

Kurkuri Bhindi

Crispy Okra

TIME TAKEN: 1 HOUR | SERVES 4

Crispy, spice coated okra makes for a delicious tea-time snack. It can also be served with a roti-subzi or a dal-rice meal, adding texture and flavour to a simple meal. Okra is traditionally deep fried to make kurkuri bhindi, but the oil tends to get a lot of spice and flour residue, making it unsuitable for a second use. Baking in the oven tends to take longer, but is less messier.

Ingredients

400 g okra / lady's fingers
3 tbsp (30 g) gram flour
1 tbsp rice flour (or cornstarch)
1 tsp salt
1 tsp ground coriander
1 tsp ground cumin
1 tsp red chilli powder
¾ tsp ground turmeric
½ tsp chaat masala
2 tbsp peanut oil

Method

1. Preheat the oven at 180°C.
2. Line a large baking tray with foil brushed with some oil.
3. If you have a smaller oven, you may need to divide the baking in two batches.
4. Wash the okra. Dry well using a towel. Top and tail the okra. Slit in half vertically. If the okra are long, then cut the vertical halves into two pieces. The pieces should be 2-3 inches long.
5. In a large bowl, mix the gram flour, rice flour, salt, ground coriander, ground cumin, red chilli powder, ground turmeric, and chaat masala. Pour oil in this mixture and combine to make a paste. Combine the okra and the spice mix. Add a teaspoon of water if need be to coat all the okra uniformly with the spice mix.
6. Transfer the okra pieces to the lined baking tray and arrange it in a single layer. Insert the baking tray in the centre of the oven and bake for 30 minutes. Halfway through the baking time, turn the baking tray around and continue baking. Okra should be crisp at the end of baking time. If not, reduce temperature to 160°C and continue baking for another 5-10 minutes depending on the desired crispness. Serve hot.

- *The spice coated okra can be deep fried in batches in 2 cups of hot oil. Deep-fry in small batches so as to not overcrowd the pan. After 1-2 minutes on high heat, reduce the heat to medium and continue frying for 2-3 minutes until golden and crisp.*
- *The same recipe can be tried using zucchini or bell pepper strips. Don't use zucchini with seeds in them.*

Papeete Ki Chutney

Green Papaya Condiment

TIME TAKEN: 15 MINUTES | SERVES 4

This chutney is traditionally served with Gujarati farsan (snacks) like fafda and khaman. One would think what good could come out of something rather bland like a green papaya, that too a condiment, which needs to have a punch of flavours. Somehow, adding just a handful of ingredients like asafoetida, green chillies, and simple spices infuses flavour into the mild tasting raw papaya, making it totally condiment worthy. Adding some gram flour to this chutney makes it robust enough to be served as a side dish to rotis or to eat along with dal and rice.

Ingredients

½ small (200 g) raw papaya
1 tbsp cooking oil
½ tsp cumin seeds
¼ tsp mustard seeds
3 green chillies, sliced
Pinch of asafoetida
¼ tsp ground turmeric
1 tsp salt
1 tsp sugar
2 tbsp gram flour
½ lime, juiced

Method

1. Peel the skin of the raw papaya. Discard the immature seeds and scrape out the pith. Using the peeler, make thin strips out of the piece of raw papaya. It can also be grated using the coarse side of the box grater.
2. Heat the oil in a pan over medium heat. Add the cumin and mustard seeds. Once the mustard splutters, fry the sliced chillies and asafoetida for a few seconds.
3. To this, add the thin strips of raw papaya (or coarsely grated), ground turmeric, salt, and sugar. Turn the heat to high and toss over for 2-3 minutes until the papaya starts to look translucent.
4. Stir in the gram flour and sprinkle some water (1-2 tablespoons) so that the flour coats all of the papaya. Reduce the heat and stir for 3-4 minutes until the flour is cooked.
5. Finish with the lime juice. Serve hot or cold as a salad, side dish with rotis or as an accompaniment to deep-fried Gujarat snacks like fafda/jalebi/dhokla.

Aam Kashundi

Green Mango and Mustard Sauce

PREP TIME: 1-2 HOURS; TIME TAKEN: 10 MINUTES;
FERMENTING TIME (OPTIONAL): 2 DAYS | MAKES OVER 1 CUP

This quintessential Bengali condiment with its golden yellow colour and the right balance of sweet, sour, heat, and pungency is sure to shine in any thali. It makes the salivary juices going, while also complementing almost every item on the plate. It does go best with Kolkata style street food like kathi rolls.

Ingredients

1 tbsp black mustard seeds
1 tbsp yellow mustard seeds
1 medium sized (200 g) raw mango
   (1 cup, chopped)
4 green chillies, sliced
1 tbsp sugar
1 tsp salt
2 tbsp mustard oil

Method

1. Soak the black and yellow mustard seeds in half a cup of water for 1-2 hours.
2. Peel and chop the raw mango into small pieces, scraping off all the flesh from the stone. Discard the stone.
3. In a mixer jar, combine the chopped raw mango, drained mustard seeds, chillies, sugar, and salt. Blend to get a fine puree. Pour the oil into this paste and pulse a couple of times until you get a creamy sauce.
4. Transfer this to a clean dry glass jar. Close loosely with a lid and allow to sit on the counter for a couple of days for it to ferment slightly. Close the lid tightly and refrigerate. This will easily stay for 2-3 weeks.

Tomato Thokku

Tamil-style Instant Tomato Pickle

TIME TAKEN: 40 MINUTES | MAKES 1½ CUPS

The Grand Sweets stores in Chennai are my favourite brand of store-bought tomato thokku. This is not always available in Bengaluru, where I live. This recipe is my attempt to recreate the taste by going through the ingredients on the label of the bottle and matching it with my memory of the flavours. A spoonful of thokku with chilled curd rice is the perfect summer lunch. In winters, mix it into steamed rice and a generous tempering of peanuts, and a Tamil homestyle tomato rice awaits you.

Ingredients

1 tsp fenugreek seeds
1 tsp cumin seeds
1 tsp + 2 tsp black mustard seeds
¼ tsp asafoetida
8 medium sized (750 g) ripe red tomatoes
1 tbsp tamarind paste
1 tsp ground turmeric
2 tsp salt
2 tbsp red chilli powder (depending on the heat)
6 tbsp Indian sesame oil (gingelly)

Method

1. In a pan over low heat, toast the fenugreek seeds, cumin seeds, and mustard seeds until the fenugreek turns a shade darker and the cumin is aromatic. Remove, cool, and grind to a powder in a spice grinder. Add the asafoetida to this mixture and keep aside.
2. Chop the tomatoes to 1-2 cm sized pieces.
3. In the same pan, combine the tomatoes, tamarind paste, ground turmeric, and salt.

Cover and allow this to simmer for 15-20 minutes over high heat until the tomatoes are pulpy and cooked. In these 15-20 minutes, check on the tomatoes at least 2-3 times (lower the heat, lift the cover and give it a stir to ensure that the paste is not sticking to the bottom of the pan).

4. Continue simmering for another 3-5 minutes until all the moisture is evaporated. Keeping the pan closed helps prevent sputtering of tomato puree outside the pan.
5. Add the prepared spice powder to this reduced puree. Stir well to combine.
6. Make a well in the centre of the pan and add the red chilli powder in the well.
7. In another pan, heat the oil. Fry the remaining mustard seeds until they pop. Once the popping sounds stop, transfer the oil to the centre of the pan over the chilli powder and stir quickly to incorporate into the thokku. Allow to cool in the pan and transfer to a clean glass jar.
8. Refrigerate the jar and use a clean dry spoon to serve the thokku.

Main Course

Gujarati Bharelu Shaak

Stuffed Brinjals and Potatoes

TIME TAKEN: 45 MINUTES | SERVES 4-6

A simple yet delicious vegetable that is made with small brinjals that make an appearance in the summer.

Ingredients

FOR FILLING
1 cup (150 g) peanuts
3 tbsp white sesame seeds
3 tbsp desiccated coconut
2 tbsp ground coriander
1 tsp red chilli powder
2 tsp jaggery
2 tsp oil
2 tbsp chopped fresh coriander
1 tsp salt

----

3 medium sized onions
2 medium sized potatoes
8 small (200 g) brinjals
1 tbsp peanut oil
Pinch of asafoetida
1 tsp cumin seeds

GARNISH
1 tbsp chopped fresh coriander

Method

1. In a pan over medium heat, roast the peanuts for 6-8 minutes until crisp. Remove the skins by rubbing peanuts between the palms. Discard the skins. Alternatively, buy roasted peanuts without the skins.
2. In the same pan, toast the sesame seeds until they start popping.
3. In a blender jar, combine the roasted peanuts and sesame seeds along with the remaining filling ingredients. Pulse to get a coarse powder. Remove to a large dish. Half the quantity is enough for this recipe. You can freeze the rest in an airtight container.
4. Peel the onion and potato. Retain the stem of the baby brinjals. Make two slits in the vegetables making a cross mark, going all along the length but not entirely. Stuff the slit vegetables with the prepared spice mix. In a heavy-bottomed pressure pan, heat 1 tablespoon oil. Add asafoetida and cumin seeds. Gently transfer the stuffed vegetables in the pan and sauté for 1-2 minutes. Add the remaining spice mix to the pan and 1 cup water. Season with salt and stir gently to combine.
5. Close the lid of the pressure cooker and after one whistle (full pressure), reduce the heat and cook for 3 minutes on the lowest heat setting. Turn off the heat. Open when pressure releases. Garnish with fresh coriander.

- *The stuffing masala can be prepared in larger quantities and saved in the freezer. This can be used to stuff any other vegetables like large chillies (banana peppers), bell peppers, and pointed gourd.*
- *It can also be used to add flavour to dry subzis like potatoes, carrot, cauliflower, zucchini, and so on. Sprinkle 2-3 tablespoons of the spice mix when the vegetables are cooked and toss well to coat.*

Ishtu

Kerala Vegetable Stew

COOKING TIME: 30 MINUTES | SERVES 4

Ingredients

1 tbsp + 1 tbsp coconut oil
2 green cardamoms
3-4 cloves
1 piece cinnamon (1")
5-6 black peppercorns
20 g ginger, julienned
1 sprig curry leaves
1 large onion, peeled and sliced
1 large carrot, peeled and diced
2 medium potatoes, peeled and diced
½ cup (60 g) green peas
12-14 green beans, julienned
1½ tsp salt
½ tsp white pepper powder (optional)
400 ml coconut milk
2 green chillies, slit
1 sprig curry leaves

Method

1. In a pan or a pressure cooker, heat the oil. Add the whole spices and fry for 30 seconds until aromatic.
2. Add half the julienned ginger and the curry leaves. Fry until the curry leaves turn bright green.
3. Stir in the sliced onions and fry over medium heat for 3-4 minutes until it softens a bit.
4. Mix in the remaining vegetables and sauté for a few seconds. Add in half a cup of water, salt, and white pepper powder. Pressure cook for 1 whistle on stove top cooker / 10 minutes in electronic pressure cooker (pressure cook mode). Release pressure.
5. Add in the coconut milk, green chillies, and the remaining ginger. Bring to a gentle simmer. Take the pan off the heat. Add a final layer of flavour with coconut oil and raw curry leaves. Serve hot with plain rice, lacy aapams, or string hoppers.

- *Some recipes do not use the whole spices and the flavouring is from ginger, chillies, curry leaves, and coconut milk alone. Spices like cardamom, cloves, and cinnamon are abundantly grown in Kerala, especially the Malabar region, so it makes sense to use it in the recipe for added flavour. You can by all means make a simpler version of this recipe by avoiding the whole spices.*
- *This recipe uses a total of 400 grams of chopped vegetables. Mix and match using the fresh vegetables that you have on hand.*

Dahi Baigana

Odia-style Baby Brinjals in Yoghurt

TIME TAKEN: 30 MINUTES | SERVES 4

I was introduced to this dish for the first time in a thali at the Jagannath temple in Bengaluru. While the entire prashad thali was delicious, this dish was a standout. It is now a regular at our home.

Ingredients

4-6 medium sized (350 g) brinjals
1 tsp Kashmiri red chilli powder
½ tsp ground cumin
½ tsp ground turmeric
½ tsp salt
4 tbsp + 2 tsp mustard oil
1½ cups (400 g) thick yoghurt
1 tsp black salt
1 tsp sugar
1 tsp cumin seeds
1 tsp panch phoron*
1 sprig curry leaves
2-3 dried red chillies

Method

1. Slice the crowns of the brinjals. Cut into quarters or wedges. In a bowl, rub the brinjal pieces with chilli powder, ground cumin, ground turmeric, and salt. Set aside for 10 minutes.
2. In a heavy flat-bottomed pan (preferably cast iron), heat 4 tablespoon of mustard oil. When the oil is hot enough, place the brinjal pieces in a single layer. Cover the pan and cook over medium heat for 3-4 minutes. The surface touching the pan will turn golden brown and the brinjal will be partially cooked. Now turn all the brinjal pieces and brown the other side evenly. Keep the heat on medium, cover and cook for another 3-4 minutes. Remove the lid and turn the brinjal pieces so they are skin side down. Cook for another 3-4 minutes. Remove the pieces to a dish to cool.
3. Meanwhile, place the yoghurt in a large bowl. Add ¼ cup water, black salt, and sugar. Whisk well.
4. In a pan over medium heat, dry roast the cumin seeds until aromatic. Remove from heat, cool, and crush using a mortar pestle to get a coarse powder. To make the tempering, in the same pan, heat the remaining mustard oil. Fry the panch phoron, curry leaves, and dried red chillies for a few seconds.
5. To assemble the dish, transfer the brinjal pieces carefully into the yoghurt. Top with prepared tempering and roasted cumin powder. Serve with hot steamed rice.

* *Panch phoron is a mix of five whole spices used in Bengali and Odia cuisines. It contains equal parts of mustard seeds, fenugreek seeds, fennel seeds, nigella seeds, and black cumin seeds (sometimes wild celery seeds/radhuni). Instead of this, you may use ½ tsp of mustard seeds alone.*

Ripe Mango Curry

TIME TAKEN: 30 MINUTES | SERVES 4

This mango curry is best made using the smallest variety of mangoes, usually the foraged ones. Here, I have used a rare variety called 'shakkar guthli', which is said to be from the Nizam era in present-day Telangana state. These fruits are very small, each weighing just under 50 grams. You can use a large variety of mango in this recipe by cutting it into quarters or bite-sized chunks.

Ingredients

8 small sized (400 g) ripe mangoes
1 tbsp tamarind (or use 1 tsp tamarind paste)
1 tbsp coconut oil
½ tsp fenugreek seeds
½ tsp mustard seeds
4 dried red chillies
2 sprigs curry leaves
½ tsp ground turmeric
½-1 tsp red chilli powder (use Kashmiri variety for lesser heat and bright colour)
1-2 tbsp powdered jaggery (or use soft brown sugar)
1 tsp salt
1 tsp rice flour (or cornstarch) [optional]

Method

1. Make a small nick at the stem end of the mangoes and pull off the peels using fingers. Soak the peels in a bowl with 1 cup water.
2. Crush the peels in the bowl of water, extracting every bit of pulp stuck to them. Squeeze out well and discard the peels. Reserve the mango water.
3. Soak the tamarind in ½ cup hot water for 5-10 minutes. Squeeze out all the pulp and reserve it.
4. Heat the oil in a frying pan. Fry the fenugreek seeds, mustard seeds, and red chillies for 30 seconds.
5. Add the curry leaves and fry until bright green and crisp.
6. To this, add the peeled mangoes and toss over high heat for 1-2 minutes.
7. Pour in the reserved mango peel water and the tamarind pulp (or paste). Stir in the ground turmeric, chilli powder, jaggery powder, and salt. Stir to combine well. Bring this to a simmer.
8. Cover the pan with a lid and allow the mixture to simmer for 10 minutes so that the mangoes absorb the flavours from all the spices. Let the curry base thicken. If you want a thicker sauce, make a slurry of rice flour in 1 tbsp water and add it to the simmering sauce with constant stirring. Remove into a serving bowl and serve with steamed rice.

- *You can prepare the same curry using pineapple chunks.*

Baingan Chokha

Smoky Eggplant Mash

TIME TAKEN: 20 MINUTES | SERVES 4

A smoky side dish from Bihar served with baked dough balls called litti. These are also made with potatoes, or a combination of brinjal and potatoes.

Ingredients

2 large (600 g) brinjals (bharta variety)
3 medium tomatoes
1 tsp mustard oil
6 cloves garlic
4 green chillies
1 tsp grated ginger
1 medium-sized onion, finely chopped
2-3 tbsp chopped fresh coriander
1 tbsp mustard oil
1 tsp salt
Juice of half a lime

Method

1. Rub the brinjals and tomatoes with mustard oil on the outside. Make a few slits with the pointed end of the knife and insert the garlic cloves into the slits. Make 2 long slits on each brinjal and insert the chilli into the slit.
2. Roast the vegetables on an open flame until charred on the outside and the brinjal is cooked inside. Inserting a cake tester or a knife will help knowing if the brinjal is soft inside.
3. Once cool, peel the brinjal and tomatoes and place in a bowl with all the remaining ingredients except mustard oil. Using hands or a masher, combine the ingredients to get a coarse mash. Drizzle the mustard oil and stir to combine.
4. Serve with rotis or a spread on a slice of sourdough bread.

- *Charred and peeled eggplant can be used in multiple ways in Indian cooking. Make baingan bharta by adding the flesh to a onion-tomato-ginger-garlic masala along with dried spices like ground coriander, red chilli powder, turmeric, and some garam masala.*
- *The mashed eggplant flesh can be mixed with yoghurt and a simple tempering of mustard seeds, red chillies, and curry leaves to make raita.*
- *Add the chopped up eggplant flesh to a tamarind-based curry with sambar powder and a tempering of mustard seeds, curry leaves, red chillies, and asafoetida to make gothsu, that can be had with rice.*

Madra

Himachali Chickpeas and Yoghurt Curry

PREP TIME: 8-10 HOURS;
COOKING TIME: 30 MINUTES | SERVES 6

A fragrant chickpea curry from Himachal Pradesh with none of the usual suspects like ginger, garlic, onion, and tomatoes that are a staple in many gravies in North India. You can also try this as a hearty soup with some crusty bread.

Ingredients

1 cup (200 g) white chickpeas, dry (kabuli chana)*
¼ tsp baking soda
2 tbsp ghee
1 tsp cumin seeds
1 pinch asafoetida
1 stick cinnamon
½ tsp ground turmeric
1 tsp red chilli powder
1 tbsp ground coriander
1½ tsp salt
1½ cup (300 g) yoghurt
1 tsp rice flour (or all-purpose flour/maida)**

FOR SPICE POWDER
2 black cardamoms
5-6 cloves
½ tsp black peppercorns
1 stick cinnamon

Method

1. Wash and soak the chickpeas in plenty of water overnight.
2. Drain the water and add chickpeas to the pressure cooker with 4 cups of water. Sprinkle baking soda into the cooking water. Close the cooker lid with the weight on. After the first whistle (or full pressure), reduce the heat and cook for 15 minutes. Turn off the heat and open the cooker when the pressure has released.
3. To prepare the spice powder: remove the seeds of the black cardamom. In a mortar, combine them with cloves, black peppercorns, and cinnamon. Crush to a coarse powder.
4. Heat 1 tablespoon ghee in a pan and fry the cumin seeds for a few seconds. Stir in the asafoetida and cinnamon.
5. Add the prepared spice powder and stir over low heat for a few seconds until its aromas are released. Add the ground turmeric, coriander, and red chilli powder along with a spoon of water. Fry for a few seconds.
6. Tip in the chickpeas with the cooking liquid. Bring it to a simmer and cook for 4-5 minutes until the chickpeas absorb the flavours of the spices.
7. Meanwhile, in a bowl, whisk the yoghurt with the rice flour until free of lumps.
8. While the chickpea curry is simmering, add the yoghurt and stir to combine. Bring this back to a gentle simmer and garnish with the remaining tablespoon of ghee. Serve hot with rice or rotis.

* *You can also use canned (cooked) chickpeas. One drained can has roughly 250 grams of cooked chickpeas. You will need around 400 grams of cooked chickpeas for this recipe.*
** *I have added rice flour to the yoghurt to prevent it from splitting. You can also add gram flour or all-purpose flour.*

Ragda Patties

Potato Patties with Dried Peas Curry

PREP TIME: 8-10 HOURS;
COOKING TIME: 45 MINUTES | SERVES 4

Ingredients

FOR RAGDA
1½ cups (250 g) dried white peas (soak overnight)
½ tsp baking soda
1 tbsp oil
Pinch of asafoetida
1 tsp cumin seeds
1 tbsp ginger-garlic paste
½ tsp ground turmeric
1 tbsp ground coriander
2 tsp ground cumin
1 tsp red chilli powder
1½ tsp salt

FOR PATTIES
4-5 medium potatoes
2 tbsp chopped fresh coriander
1 tsp salt
½ tsp ground turmeric
1 tsp amchoor powder
1-2 green chillies, finely chopped
3-4 tbsp oil to fry the patties

TO SERVE
Green chutney
Tamarind chutney
Chopped onions
Fresh coriander leaves
Lime wedges

Method

1. To prepare ragda: Take the overnight soaked peas and discard the soaking water. Transfer this to a pressure cooker. Add 3 cups of water and baking soda. Close the lid and bring it to full pressure (one whistle). Reduce the heat to low and continue cooking for 3-4 minutes.

2. In a pan, heat 1 tablespoon oil. Fry the asafoetida and cumin seeds. Once the seeds sizzle, add the ginger-garlic paste and cook for a minute or two over low heat. Add the turmeric, coriander, cumin, and red chilli powder along with a splash of water. Let this fry for 30 seconds.

3. Transfer the cooked peas mixture in the pressure cooker to this pan. Season with salt and let it simmer for 4-5 minutes. Thin down with some hot water to keep the ragda to a pouring consistency.

4. To prepare patties: Pressure cook or boil the potatoes. Peel and mash or grate them to get a lump-free texture. Lightly knead the potatoes, coriander, salt, turmeric, amchoor, and green chillies until it comes together.

5. Divide into 8 portions and shape into a ball. Flatten it to 2 cm thickness. Roll it like a wheel on a board or the counter to get smoothened outside.

6. Take 1-2 tbsp oil on a large flat skillet or a pan. Once the oil is hot, fry the patties on one side for 4-5 minutes over medium heat. Flip over to the other side, spoon some oil along the sides and cook this side for another 4-5 minutes until golden brown on the outside.

ASSEMBLE A PLATE

7. In a small deep dish, place two pieces of patties. Top with a cup of ragda. Spoon some of the green chutney and tamarind chutney over the ragda. Sprinkle 1-2 spoons of finely chopped onions and a bit of chopped coriander. Serve with a wedge of lime. This dish is served warm or hot.

Jolada Dosa

Sorghum Dosa

PREP TIME: 14 HOURS, INCLUDING FERMENTING TIME;
COOKING TIME: 20 MINUTES | SERVES 4

I ate jolada dosa for the first time at Malabar Restaurant, an eatery started in 1944 in Balapet, Bengaluru. It was one of their specials and available only on one day of the week. A hot selling item, if you went in later in the day, they would run out of this batter and the dish would no longer be available. Sadly, the eatery shut down in 2013 after being in the business for 79 years.

Ingredients

½ cup (100 g) black gram (skinned split urad dal)
1 tbsp fenugreek seeds
½ cup (35 g) flattened rice
¼ cup (60 g) yoghurt
1 cup (135 g) sorghum flour
1½ tsp salt

TO PREPARE A DOSA
1 small onion, chopped
2 tbsp chopped coriander
1 green chilli, chopped
¼ tsp chopped ginger
5-6 curry leaves, chopped
Pinch of ground turmeric (optional)
1-2 tsp oil

Method

1. Wash and soak the black gram along with fenugreek seeds for 3-4 hours.
2. Soak the poha in half cup water and yoghurt for 30 minutes.
3. In a blender jar, take the drained soaked lentils and the soaked poha. Add in the sorghum flour and blend to get a smooth paste, adding some of the soaking water if required. The consistency should be like pancake batter. Remove the batter to a bowl. Mix in the salt with your hands. Cover and keep aside for 6-10 hours until the batter is well fermented (almost doubled in volume and lots of air bubbles when you scoop the batter with a ladle).
4. At this point, you can either refrigerate the batter or prepare the dosas.
5. A flat cast iron or non-stick griddle is required for making the dosas.
6. For each dosa, use around $1/3$ cup batter. Add the chopped onion, coriander, chillies, ginger, and curry leaves. Stir well and pour over a lightly greased hot griddle. Drizzle oil around the edges and allow to cook for 2-3 minutes over medium heat until golden on the underside. Flip over and cook for another 2-3 minutes. Serve hot with tomato thokku.

Gavar Dhokli

Cluster Beans with Sorghum Pasta

TIME TAKEN: 50 MINUTES | SERVES 4

My version of a Gujarati pasta dish that can be eaten as is.

Ingredients

FOR THE DHOKLI/PASTA
¾ cup (100 g) sorghum flour
¼ cup (40 g) gram flour
¼ tsp ground turmeric
½ tsp sugar
2 tsp groundnut oil
¼ cup (12 g) chopped coriander leaves
4 cloves garlic
4 green chillies
1 tsp salt

FOR THE BEANS/GUVAR
300 grams tender cluster beans
2 tsp groundnut oil
1 tsp cumin seeds
¼ tsp asafoetida
1 tsp ginger-green chilli paste
¼ tsp ground turmeric
1 tsp sugar
¾ tsp salt

FOR GARNISH
1 tsp toasted white sesame seeds
2 tbsp finely chopped fresh coriander

Method

1. To prepare the dhokli (pasta) dough: In a small bowl, mix together flours, ground turmeric, sugar, and oil. Using a mortar pestle, crush the coriander, garlic, green chillies, and salt to a coarse paste. Combine the flours and paste using a little warm water and bind into a stiff dough. Cover and keep aside for 10 minutes.

2. To prepare the beans, slice off the two ends. As we are using the tender variety, you wont need to remove the fibrous string on both sides. Cut the prepared beans into 1 inch long pieces.

3. In a pan, heat the oil and fry cumin seeds. After a few seconds, add asafoetida, ginger-green chilli paste, ground turmeric, and chopped beans. Season with salt and sugar and stir over medium heat for 1-2 minutes. Keep a small pan of water to boil on the side. Add half cup boiling hot water to the beans in the pan. Cover and allow to simmer for 7-8 minutes until nearly cooked.

4. While the beans are cooking, divide the prepared dough into 30 portions. Flatten out each one to around ½ cm thickness. This is the dhokli. Add 2 cups of boiling hot water to the cooked beans in the pan and gently drop in all the dhokli into the boiling water. Simmer for 8-10 minutes.

5. Taste a dhokli to check for doneness. There should be no raw floury taste when you bite into it.

6. If you want the dish to have more liquid, add little extra water and simmer for a minute. Divide between four bowls and garnish with some toasted sesame seeds and chopped fresh coriander. Serve hot.

Sweets

Mango Phirni

Mango and Cream of Wheat Pudding

PREP TIME: 20 MINUTES; COOKING TIME: 10 MINUTES;
REFRIGERATION TIME: 3-4 HOURS | SERVES 4

Phirni is a popular pudding prepared in the North Indian cuisine. It is easy to make and less time consuming as compared to kheer. A basic phirni is made using just ground rice. Addition of seasonal fruits like mangoes makes it a treat for mango lovers. This version uses rava instead of rice.

Ingredients

3 tbsp granulated wheat /
   semolina (rava/sooji)
3 cups (750 ml) full cream milk
Pinch of saffron strands
¼ cup (50 g) sugar
1 large (400 g) ripe mango
2 tbsp chopped pistachios

Method

1. Soak the rava in ½ cup of milk for 15-20 minutes and keep aside.
2. Bring the milk to boil in a heavy saucepan.
3. Take the saffron strands in a small cup and add 2-3 tablespoons of hot milk to it.
4. Reduce the heat and, to the simmering milk, add the soaked rava and sugar, stirring constantly. In 5-7 minutes, the milk will thicken as the rava gets fully cooked.
5. Remove from the heat and keep aside. It will thicken further on cooling.
6. Meanwhile, peel, chop, and puree the mango. Stir the mango puree into the cooled milk mixture. Divide between 4-6 small earthen pots or dessert cups.
7. Garnish with chopped pistachios. Cover each pot with foil to prevent drying out and refrigerate for 3-4 hours before serving.

• *Select a sweet and non-fibrous variety of mango. Imampasand or Alphonso are good varieties to use in this dessert. Use 2 mangoes if using Alphonso as these mangoes are smaller in size.*

Thinai Payasam

Foxtail Millet Pudding

PREP TIME: 1-2 HOURS; COOKING TIME: 1 HOUR I SERVES 4-6

Millet is an ancient grain with different varieties grown all over India. There is a resurgence of millets all over the country due to growing awareness of their health benefits. Millets are not just used in place of rice to eat with cooked lentils or curries, but also to make desserts. Millet doesn't turn as mushy and creamy as rice, giving the kheer a unique texture. I find that the foxtail millet variety is best suited to kheers.

Ingredients

¼ cup (50 g) foxtail millet (kangni)
1 litre full cream milk
½ cup (100 g) raw cane sugar
Pinch of saffron strands

Method

1. Wash and soak the millet in a bowl of water for 1-2 hours. Drain and keep aside.
2. In a pressure cooker (electronic or stovetop), add the milk, sugar, and soaked millet.
3. In an electronic pressure cooker, set the menu to Pressure Cooking → High Pressure → 40 minutes. Once the time is up and the pressure lowers, open the lid, add the saffron strands, and put it back in the pressure cook setting for 10 minutes.
4. In the stove top pressure cooker, combine ingredients and allow to come to full pressure over high heat. Reduce the heat and keep for 30-40 minutes on lowest heat. Once the pressure lowers, open the lid, add the saffron strands, and put it back in the pressure cook setting for 10 minutes. Make sure this pressure cooker has a heavy bottom or a long period of pressure cooking could burn the milk.
5. Millet payasam is ready to be served hot or cold.

• *Fry 1-2 tablespoons of cashews and raisins in 2 tablespoons of ghee for an optional garnish.*

Aamrakhand

Sweetened Mango Yoghurt

TIME TAKEN: 15 MINUTES | SERVES 4

This is a dessert served as a part of the main meal in Maharashtrian cuisine. Eaten along with hot puri, it is one of summer's delicacies. In Maharashtra, dairy shops sell hung yoghurt called chakka. It is easily made at home by straining full cream yoghurt.

Ingredients

1 cup (250 g) hung yoghurt*
2 cups (250 g) powdered sugar
2-3 tbsp whole milk
½ cup (130 g) thick mango pulp
¼ tsp ground green cardamom seeds
Few strands of saffron
1 tsp chopped pistachios

Method

1. Keep a fine meshed strainer over a bowl. Transfer the hung yoghurt to the strainer. Using a silicone spatula, rub the yoghurt so that creamy yoghurt with smooth consistency gets collected in the bowl below.
2. Put the strainer aside.
3. Add the sugar to the bowl and, using a wooden spoon or fork, whisk the yoghurt-sugar mixture for 4-5 minutes, until well combined and fluffy. Use milk by the spoonful to get a smooth consistency that resembles a cream cheese frosting.
4. Tip in the mango pulp into this bowl along with ground green cardamom and whisk once again until well combined and fluffy.
5. Transfer to a serving bowl. Garnish with saffron strands and pistachios.
6. Serve with hot puris.

- *Aamrakhand can also be used as a topping over mango-based desserts like bars, muffins, and cakes.*
- *Similar fruit-based shrikhand can be prepared using other seasonal fruits like strawberry, orange, and pineapple.*
- *Take care not to add any water or liquid to the peeled and chopped mango pieces while making a pulp.*
- *Each 400 gram tub of store-bought thick yoghurt gives 150-200 grams of hung yoghurt.*

Lauki Halwa

Bottle Gourd Fudge

TIME TAKEN: 30 MINUTES | SERVES 4

Vegetables of the gourd variety are commonly used to prepare sweets in Indian cuisine. Kasi halwa in Tamil cuisine made using ash gourd, stuffed pointed gourd sweet in Bengali cuisine, petha made from ash gourd that the city of Agra is famous for, are some of the examples.

Ingredients

1 tbsp ghee
2 cups (400 g) grated bottle gourd
½ cup (100 g) raw cane sugar
½ cup (100 g) grated khoya
¼ tsp ground green cardamom

FOR GARNISH
2-3 tsp sliced almonds
Few strands of saffron

Method

1. Heat ghee in a heavy-bottomed pan.
2. Add the grated bottle gourd and stir continuously over low to medium heat for 3-4 minutes.
3. Reduce the heat to low; cover and steam cook for 6-8 minutes until the bottle gourd is softened.
4. Uncover the pan and allow the excess moisture to dry out.
5. Mix in the grated khoya and sugar and keep stirring. The khoya and sugar will start melting. After 5-6 minutes of stirring, the entire mixture will come together.
6. Once all the excess moisture is dried out, mix in the cardamom powder.
7. Transfer to a serving bowl and garnish with slivered or sliced almonds and a few strands of saffron.

- *Blanch a handful of spinach leaves and grind it to a puree in the mixer jar. Take this in a muslin cloth and squeeze gently to extract spinach juice. About 2-3 tablespoons of the juice can be added to the halwa when it is almost done to give it a vibrant green colour.*
- *You can also divide the halwa into 8 portions, roll it into balls, garnish each portion with a pinch of almonds and a saffron strand. Serve these in individual small cups or in paper liners.*

monsoon

Monsoon is the most dramatic season in India. The northeast monsoon winds blow from land to sea during cooler months. The southwest monsoon winds blow during the warmest months of the year, from sea to land crossing the Indian Ocean, Arabian Sea, and the Bay of Bengal. These winds are responsible for most of the rains in India, through the months of June and August. Kharif crops are sown just before the start of the southwest monsoons and harvested towards the end of the monsoons. Rice, corn, millets, sorghum, sugarcane, tur dal, urad dal, ground nuts, gourds, tomatoes, turmeric are some of the crops harvested during this period.

Monsoon in the Indian peninsula

In most parts of India, when it rains, it pours. The city of Mumbai is a good example of this. An umbrella is no good if you are caught in one of these downpours. Born and brought up in erstwhile Bombay, June meant only two things – reopening of the school and the monsoons. School reopening had its own set of preparations like getting new books, uniforms, bag, shoes, umbrellas, gum boots, raincoats, etc. organized.

Such rained-out days can be enjoyed from a window or a balcony, watching sheets of water come down on whatever view one's house affords, with hot ginger chai, deep-fried pakodas or a plate of khichdi billowing steam into which a spoonful of ghee is melting away.

Khichuri, a dish that the British took back home as kedgeree, is a savoury porridge made using dal, rice, and spices. This is a rainy-day favourite of many a Bengali. Khichuri could be of varying consistencies, from soupy to fluffy, plain or with seasonal vegetables and spices, depending on the mood of the cook and is served with deep-fried slices of eggplant (begun bhaja), or crispy shoestring potato fries (jhuri jhuri aloo bhaja).

In Kerala, there is a special monsoon gruel called karikada kanji (karikaradam being the name of the month that receives the maximum rainfall). The main ingredient used in this gruel is the native red rice (GI tagged njavara rice) and a mix of ten powdered herbs. This healthy gruel is cooked with black pepper, cumin and fenugreek, along with coconut milk, and jaggery. It is served as part of Ayurvedic treatment sessions conducted during monsoons.

The most awaited festival in Kerala, Onam, also falls during the rains. A harvest festival to celebrate the bounty from the monsoons, the Onam sadhya (a vegetarian feast served on a banana leaf) showcases all the fresh produce of the season with over twenty-one dishes. Crispy fried vegetable chips (plantain or yam), jaggery coated sweet chips, puffy fried pappadam, a variety of pickles, yoghurt-based curries, coconut and spice-based curries, simple vegetable stir-fries and milk or coconut milk-based puddings are the dishes served in a sadhya.

In Western India, monsoons usher community festivals such as Nag Pacham (a day to worship snakes), Shital Satam (a day to give rest to the hearth and eat only cold foods), and Randhan Chhath (a day to worship fire by cooking up a feast). The practice of avoiding leafy greens and sticking to seasonal gourds along with pantry staples like grains, flours, and legumes is the norm.

Crispy cravings

Eating street food during the rains might not seem like the smartest idea due to hygiene issues, and yet is irresistible. Anything spicy, deep-fried and served with a smattering of hot and sweet chutneys is a monsoon-must many Indians identify with. Deep-fried food is a favourite in streets and in homes during the rains. Samosas, onion pakodas and bajjis or bhajias made with potatoes, eggplant, plantain are all dishes you may find in an Indian home for an evening tea-time snack, or ordered in from the trusted local outlet.

Shravan

Shravan month, that, as per the Hindu calendar falls during the monsoons, is a ritual-heavy one. It is customary for meat eaters in the states of Maharashtra, Karnataka and Goa to turn vegetarian and teetotaler for this period of time, while some others practise fasting. The people along the Konkan coast who mostly eat a seafood rich diet through the year, abstain from eating fish during these months for a couple of reasons. It is rather dangerous for fishermen to venture out fishing in the choppy waters during these months. This is also the time when fish spawn, so belief has it that not eating fish during this period will allow for more fish all year round.

Aadi Perukku in Tamil Nadu

The peak of the monsoon falls during the Tamil month of Aadi with swelling rivers, freshly sowed paddy and fluorescent green paddy shoots along the river banks. Aadi Perukku is celebrated on the 18th day of the Aadi month as a mark of gratitude to the rivers and nature's bounty. My grandmother used to speak fondly of the picnic womenfolk would have on the banks of the rivers, lakes, or even around wells, when all the water bodies would be pregnant with fresh rain water. The association of this festival is with fertility and reproduction. Tamilians prepare a variety of rice preparations (at least four) such as coconut rice, lemon rice, tamarind rice, jaggery sweetened rice, and so on.

Monsoons and Ayurveda

According to Ayurveda, it is during the varsha ritu or rainy season, between July and September, when the agni (digestive fire) is most sluggish. Salty, sour and oily foods are favoured during this season, avoiding all kinds of uncooked foods with a preference for fresh hot meals. Ingredients like ginger, lemon, black pepper help boost the agni. Light, well-cooked khichdi made with rice, millets, moong are nourishing and light to digest.

Music to cook. Scan the QR Code to listen to India's most iconic monsoon raagas.

Foraged and wild produce

Early monsoon breathes a new life into soil, bringing a wide variety of bright and tender green leafy vegetables, such as dill, amaranth (both red and green), fenugreek, spinach, and drumstick leaves. In Mumbai, ingredients like takla, shevala, phodshi, ambushi and morshend are foraged from surrounding hilly areas or grown in the brackish waters near the seaside. These are relished by locals, incorporating this transient produce in their daily cooking. City folk are not aware of these hidden, wild gems, with the exception of some new, urban, home chefs who are promoting these ingredients.

SCAN ME

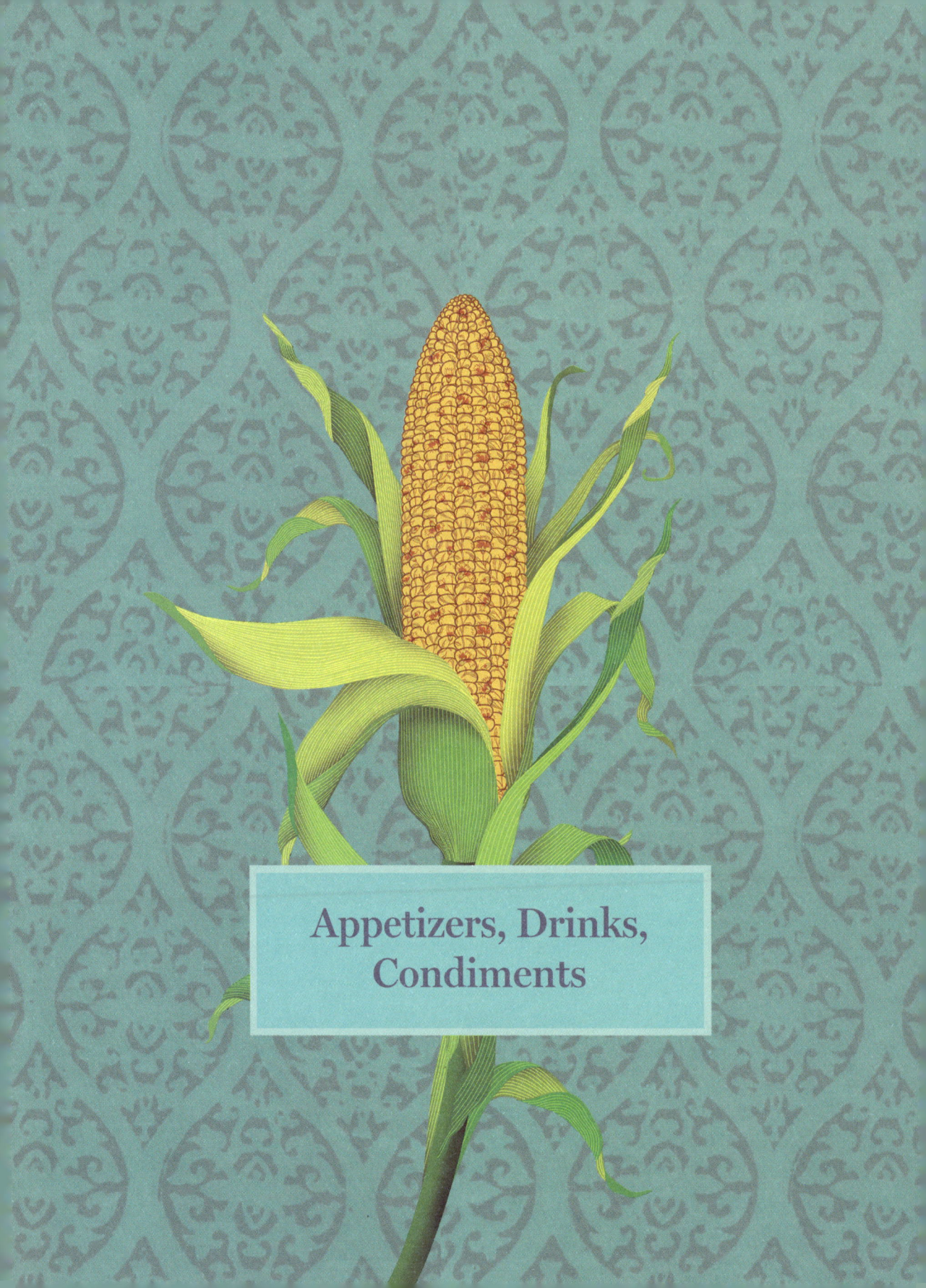

Appetizers, Drinks, Condiments

Adrak Chai

Ginger Tea

TIME TAKEN: 10 MINUTES | SERVES 4

Ingredients

4 cups water
2" (25 g) piece fresh ginger
¼ tsp ground ginger (sonth) (optional)
2 tbsp chopped lemongrass leaves (optional)
5 tsp CTC tea leaves or 5-6 tea bags
½ cup milk*
Sugar as required

Method

1. Take 4 cups of water in a saucepan. Crush the ginger coarsely using a mortar pestle and add it to the water. You can also grate the ginger finely and use that instead. Stir in ground ginger and chopped lemongrass, if using.
2. Let the water boil for 3-4 minutes so that the essence of ginger and lemongrass is extracted into the water.
3. At this point, reduce the heat and add the CTC tea. Let this simmer for 3-4 minutes.
4. Stir in the milk and allow the tea to come to boil once again. Keep covered for 2-3 minutes for a stronger brew. This is optional. Remove from heat and strain into 4 cups. Stir in sugar as per desired sweetness. One to two teaspoons per cup is ideal. Serve hot.

*	For a vegan version, use any reasonably neutral flavoured plant based milk.

Ragi Ambli

Savoury Finger Millet Porridge

TIME TAKEN: 10 MINUTES | SERVES 2

A quick and nourishing savoury breakfast.

Ingredients

4 tbsp ragi flour
1½ cups water
½ tsp salt
1 cup (250 ml) buttermilk (or thinned yoghurt)
1 small onion, finely chopped
1-2 green chillies, finely chopped
1 sprig curry leaves

Method

1. In a small cup, make a slurry of ragi flour with ½ cup of water.
2. Keep the remaining 1 cup of water to boil in a saucepan. Once the water boils, add the ragi flour slurry with constant stirring. Reduce the heat to low and simmer for 5 minutes until the mixture thickens and the flour is cooked. Season with salt.
3. Stir in the buttermilk, chopped onions, chillies, and curry leaves.
4. Divide between two bowls and serve. This can be had hot or at room temperature. The porridge will thicken on cooling.

• *You can prepare a similar porridge using jowar (sorghum flour) or any other millet flour.*
• *The porridge can be made sweet by adding milk instead of buttermilk and crushed jaggery instead of salt, onion, chilli, and curry leaves.*

Makai Ke Pakode

Sweet Corn Fritters

TIME TAKEN: 30 MINUTES | SERVES 4

The combination of sweet corn kernels mixed with chillies, ginger, and spices, coated in gram flour, and deep fried to golden perfection is an irresistible one. Each bite of the makkai pakoda satisfies the craving to eat something spicy and crunchy when the rains come lashing. Best served with steaming hot cups of ginger tea.

Ingredients

2 sweet corn on cob (200 grams shelled/1 cup)
1 small onion, finely chopped
2-3 green chillies, finely sliced
1 tsp grated ginger
¾ cup (75 g) gram flour
¼ cup (35 g) rice flour
½ tsp ground turmeric
1 tsp salt
1 tsp red chilli powder
Pinch of asafoetida
3-4 tbsp finely chopped fresh coriander
2 cups oil for deep-frying*
1 tsp chaat masala (optional)

Method

1. Slice off the corn from the cob in 3-4 layers so that the kernels are coarsely chopped and not intact. Add these to a bowl and combine with all the other ingredients except the oil for frying. Keep the oil to heat in a heavy-bottomed pan.

2. Once the oil is hot, take one tablespoon of hot oil and add to the corn mixture in the bowl. To this, add water, a little at a time, to get a thick muffin-batter like consistency. This is the pakoda batter.

3. Pick around a tablespoon of batter at a time either with a spoon or fingertips and drop into the hot oil. Keep the heat high when dropping in the batter. You can make 6-8 at a time depending on the size of the pan. Once all the pakodas are dropped, reduce the heat to medium and fry for 7-8 minutes turning them around, so that they are golden brown and crisp on the outside, and inside.

4. Sprinkle chaat masala over the pakodas and serve hot with green chutney or ketchup.

- *Add 2-3 tbsp of red or green bell pepper to the batter for pops of colour.*
- *Prepared pakodas can be kept warm in an oven that is heated at 120°C.*
- *You can also make these in the air-fryer or oven.*

Masala Vadai

Crispy Lentil Fritters

PREP TIME: 1-2 HOURS; COOKING TIME: 20 MINUTES; SERVES 4-6

These deep fried flavour and texture bombs don't need any accompaniments, but no harm dipping it in a spot of ketchup or hot and sweet sauce. Falafels from the south of India but with a flavour bomb.

Ingredients

1 cup (170 g) Bengal gram (chana dal)
1-2 dried red chillies
1 small piece (1") cinnamon stick
½ tsp fennel seeds
1 medium sized onion, finely chopped
3 cloves garlic, crushed with skins
2 green chillies, sliced
¼ cup chopped fresh coriander leaves
¼ cup mint leaves
2 sprigs curry leaves, chopped
1½ tsp salt
2 cups oil to deep-fry (rice bran or sunflower)

Method

1. Wash and soak dal for 1-2 hours.
2. Drain water thoroughly. Before grinding, keep a handful of soaked dal aside.
3. Add the remaining dal along with the red chillies, fennel seeds and cinnamon to a food processor and blend without adding any extra water to get a coarse paste.
4. Remove this into a large bowl. Add the soaked dal kept aside, chopped onions, garlic, chillies, coriander, mint, and curry leaves.
5. Season with salt and mix well with hands so that the flavouring ingredients are mixed well into the dough.
6. Divide into 15-16 portions of 25 grams each. Roll into balls between the palms.
7. Take 2 cups of oil to heat in a heavy-bottomed frying pan. Once the oil is hot, flatten each ball lightly and add it gently into the oil. Let the vadas fry undisturbed for 5 minutes over medium-high heat. They will start floating, at which point you can turn them over to the other side and continue frying for another 3-4 minutes until golden brown and crisp on the outside.

- *Do not soak dal beyond two hours for this recipe as the dals start getting fermented, giving a sour flavour to the vada.*
- *Once salt is added to the dough, start preparing the vadas immediately or the onions and herbs will lose water and make the dough wet.*
- *Depending on the size of the pan, make sure you add enough vadas to fry in one batch but not too many as that will reduce the temperature of the oil.*

Pazham Pori

Batter Fried Bananas

PREP TIME: 2-3 HOURS; COOKING TIME: 30 MINUTES | SERVES 4

A Kerala tea shop specialty prepared using local Nendran bananas, these banana fritters are a much loved accompaniment with tea. Unlike most fritters in Indian cuisine that are dipped in a gram flour batter, the batter for pazham pori is made using all-purpose flour and a touch of leftover dosa batter to give it slight fermentation and a tangy flavour.

Ingredients

1 cup (100 g) all-purpose flour
2 tbsp rice flour
2 tbsp sugar
¼ tsp salt
¼ tsp ground turmeric
2 tbsp dosa batter
4-6 ripe bananas (Nendran variety, if possible)
2 cups oil for deep-frying

Method

1. In a bowl, combine all the dry ingredients. Mix in the dosa batter. Add water, a little at a time, mixing with a wire whisk or with your fingers to make a thick batter that falls in ribbons (cake batter consistency).
2. Cover the bowl and keep aside for 2-3 hours.
3. Peel the bananas. Slice in half vertically. Depending on the size of your frying pan, you may cut each of these pieces horizontally to get 4 pieces per banana.
4. Heat the oil in a heavy-bottomed pan. Once the oil is hot, dip each piece of banana in the batter to coat it thoroughly and drop it gently into the oil. Fry 3-4 pieces at a time making sure that the pan is not overcrowded. Reduce the heat / temperature to medium and allow the coating to become golden brown all around. This should take around 5 minutes of frying. Before dropping the next batch of bananas, allow the oil to heat up properly.
5. Drain the fried bananas using a slotted spoon in a dish covered with kitchen paper to remove any excess oil.
6. Serve hot with cups of strong black tea.

- In the absence of dosa batter, use a similar quantity of thinned sourdough starter if you have that. Or else, let the prepared batter sit for 4-5 hours. Add ¼ tsp baking powder along with a spoon of water and mix well before starting the cooking process.
- In Kerala, a certain variety of bananas called Nendran is used to make this snack. You can use any other variety of ripe bananas for this if you cannot find the said variety. Bananas can be either halved and used or cut into thinner slices.

Pathravadi

Colocasia Leaf Pinwheels

TIME TAKEN: 1 HOUR | SERVES 4

Colocasia (arbi), a root vegetable, is used regularly in Indian cuisine. The leaves are dark green, thick, and edible. Use tender leaves for this recipe as mature leaves may cause itching of hands, mouth, and throat due to high calcium oxalate content. Acidic ingredients like lime and tamarind reduce this side effect.

Ingredients

5-6 (105 g) tender colocasia leaves (arbi patta)*
2 limes
2 tbsp tamarind flakes
1 cup (100 g) gram flour
2 tbsp sorghum flour (jowar atta)
2 tbsp crushed jaggery
1 tbsp white sesame seeds
2 tsp salt
2 tsp red chilli powder
2 tsp ground coriander
1 tsp ground turmeric
$^1/_8$ tsp baking soda
2 tsp peanut oil

Method

1. Wash the colocasia leaves well and drain. Slice off the stem and any thick veins carefully. In a large bowl of water, squeeze two limes and immerse the leaves for 15 minutes. This helps reduce the itchiness caused by handling the leaves. Wipe the leaves dry.

2. Boil the tamarind in 1 cup of water for 10 minutes. Extract the pulp by straining the tamarind solids and liquid.

3. In a bowl, prepare the spice paste to apply on the leaves. Combine the prepared tamarind extract along with besan, jowar, jaggery, sesame seeds, salt, red chilli powder, ground turmeric, ground coriander, baking soda, and peanut oil. Add enough water to make a thick paste.

4. On a counter, place the largest leaf with its smooth side facing down and pointed end facing away from you. Apply the paste all over the leaf. Place another leaf over this and apply the paste similarly until all the leaves and paste is used up.

5. Fold over the two long ends slightly and seal with the paste so that the ends are not open. Start rolling from the bottom end, tightly, all the way to the top. The paste helps keep the roll sealed.

6. Over medium heat, place a steamer going with roughly 1" of water in the bottom panel. Oil the steamer basket lightly. Place the roll in the steamer and steam over medium heat for 25 minutes or until a knife inserted into the roll comes out clean, indicating that the paste is cooked through. Note that not steaming the leaves well enough can also leave it partially uncooked and trigger off an allergic itch in the throat.

* *Wear gloves while touching the leaves, in case they cause itching or irritation. If colocasia leaves are not easily available, use spinach, swiss chard, kale, or other such greens.*

Main Course

Ragi Dosa

Savoury Finger Millet Crepes

COOKING TIME: 20 MINUTES | SERVES 4-6

Substitute rice with ragi or finger millet in your dosa batter for a more healthy and nutritious dish. Ragi has a higher proportion of fibre, protein and vitamins as compared to white rice. This recipe can be made using a fermented batter or an instant mix of flours.

Ingredients

1½ cups (~200 g) ragi flour
½ cup (~80 g) rice flour
¼ cup (60 g) sour yoghurt
3-4 cups water
2 tsp oil
1 tsp cumin seeds
2 green chillies, finely chopped
2 sprigs curry leaves, finely chopped
1 medium-sized onion, finely chopped
2 tsp salt
½ tsp baking soda
Oil or ghee to make dosas

Method

1. In a large bowl combine rice and ragi flour. Make a well and add the yoghurt. Whisk the yoghurt into the flours. Add 3 cups of water. Gradually add the remaining water as needed. The consistency should be of a watery soup.

2. Heat the oil in a pan over medium heat. Add the cumin seeds, green chillies, curry leaves and chopped onion and fry for 4-5 minutes until onions are soft. Add this to the batter.

3. Sprinkle baking soda on the batter and season with salt. Whisk well to combine all ingredients.

4. Heat a cast iron skillet (or non-stick pan). Smear a few drops of oil using kitchen paper or a brush on the surface of the skillet.

5. Transfer the batter to a jug and pour the batter to cover the entire skillet from a height of 6 inches or so. There will be a lot of holes on the surface. Pour 1-2 tsp oil around the dosa. Cook over medium heat for 2-3 minutes. Flip over and cook the other side briefly. Place the dosa on a plate and serve hot with a chutney of your choice.

6. Follow the same process to make more dosas using the remaining batter.

- *To make a fermented version of the ragi dosa, mix 1 cup ragi flour and ¼ cup rice flour in 1 cup water. Soak ¼ cup skinned urad dal with 1 tsp fenugreek seeds for 1 hour. Drain and grind it to a fine paste along with ½ cup water. Add the ragi-rice flour paste to the blender and combine it with the urad dal paste. Scrape out the contents into a bowl. Season with salt. Cover and ferment overnight or for 8 hours. The batter will rise and increase in volume. You can either make dosas from this immediately or refrigerate the batter until use. Bring the batter to room temperature before making the dosas. Unlike the recipe for ragi dosa given above, the consistency of this batter is thick and it needs to be spread out on the tava with the back of a ladle.*

Amrood Subzi

Guava Curry

Tropical fruits like mango, pineapple, banana, and guava quite often find themselves in spicy curries that are to be had with rice or rotis. The inherent sweetness of the fruit offset by spices gives a delightful sweet-savoury experience.

Ingredients

5 small (400 g) ripe guavas*
1 tbsp mustard oil**
½ tsp fenugreek seeds
½ tsp cumin seeds
½ tsp fennel seeds
1 tsp grated ginger
Pinch of asafoetida
1 tbsp ground coriander powder
1 tsp red chilli powder
½ tsp ground turmeric
1 tsp raw mango powder
½ tsp black salt***
½ tsp rock salt
1 tsp ginger, juliennes
2 tbsp chopped fresh coriander leaves

Method

1. Peel the guavas if the skin is too thick. Chop into halves and then quarters. Slice out most of the seeds and discard. Cut into bite sized pieces. You should get roughly two cups of chopped guava.
2. Heat the oil in a deep pan. Fry fenugreek seeds, cumin seeds, and fennel seeds for a few seconds.
3. Stir in the grated ginger and asafoetida.
4. Add the coriander powder, red chilli powder, and turmeric and fry well along with the spices for a few seconds.
5. Mix in the chopped guava, black salt, and rock salt. Sauté over high heat for 1-2 minutes.
6. Pour a cup and a half of water. Allow to come to a boil. Reduce the heat and simmer for 6-8 minutes until the guava pieces are soft and the curry has thickened.
7. At this stage, add amchoor powder and ginger juliennes. Stir to combine.
8. Garnish with fresh coriander.
9. Serve hot with puris or rotis.

* *Choose guavas that are just ripe and not overripe as overripe fruit will fall apart and turn mushy on cooking.*
** *Mustard oil provides the characteristic flavour in some of the curries in North India. You may substitute with any other cooking oil.*
*** *Black salt adds a unique flavour to the curry. You may use regular salt if you don't have this.*

Bhutte Ki Khees

Spicy Corn Mash

TIME TAKEN: 20 MINUTES

This is a famous street food from the city of Indore in Madhya Pradesh. Sarafa Bazaar in Indore is well known for its bhutte ki khees, which literally means grated corn. At home it can be had for breakfast or as a small meal. Given that it is tough to source 'desi bhutta' or local corn that is seasonal in monsoons, try with sweet corn on the cob that is available all round the year.

Ingredients

4 sweet corn on the cob (bhutta)
2 tbsp ghee or oil
Pinch of asafoetida
1 tsp mustard seeds
1 tsp cumin seeds
3-4 green chillies, sliced
2 tsp grated ginger
1 tsp salt
½ tsp ground turmeric
1 cup (250 ml) milk*
2 tbsp chopped coriander
2 tbsp grated coconut
2 tbsp lime juice

Method

1. Grate all the corn on the cobs coarsely (only the kernel layer) to get around 400 g of grated corn. Keep aside.**
2. Heat the ghee in a pan over medium heat. Stir in the asafoetida.
3. Fry mustard and cumin seeds. Once the mustard stops sputtering, add the chillies and ginger. Fry over high heat for a few seconds.
4. To this, add the grated corn and fry over medium to high heat with continuous stirring for 3-4 minutes. Stir in salt and turmeric. Mix well.
5. Pour in the milk and continue stirring until all the milk is incorporated into the corn mixture. Sauté this mixture for another 3-4 minutes over medium heat.
6. Garnish with fresh coriander, coconut, and lime juice.
7. Serve hot.

* For a dairy free option, use soy milk or oat milk as other strongly flavoured milk will change the flavour of the dish.
** Use the coarse side of the grater to grate the corn. Grating it too fine will make it a paste and the dish will lack texture.

Ajwaini Arbi

Crispy Colocasia with Carom Seeds

TIME TAKEN: 30 MINUTES | SERVES 6

Colocasia or arbi is a tricky vegetable to work with. When overcooked, it turns slimy and unappetizing. When cooked just right, tossed in spices and allowed to slow roast in some oil in a pan, it turns into a delicious side dish or appetiser. Choose arbi of similar size for this recipe so they all cook uniformly.

Ingredients

300 g colocasia (arbi) (small sized)
1 tsp salt
2 tsp ground coriander
1 tsp red chilli powder
½ tsp ground turmeric
1½ tsp carom seeds
2 tsp rice flour
2 tbsp peanut oil
½ tsp black mustard seeds
Pinch of asafoetida
2 tsp dried fenugreek leaves

Method

1. Wash and place the colocasia in a small bowl. Keep this bowl in a pressure cooker with water in it. Close the lid and pressure cook for one whistle. Turn off the heat and allow the cooker to cool. Once cooled, remove the bowl and let the cooked colocasia cool down enough to handle. Peel the skins and discard.

2. Lightly smash each cooked colocasia in your palm so it becomes flattened.
3. Keep the peeled and smashed colocasia in a dish. To this, add salt, ground coriander, red chilli powder, ground turmeric, 1 teaspoon of the carom seeds (crushed in the palm or in a mortar pestle), and rice flour. Toss gently to coat each piece evenly in the spice mix.
4. Heat the oil in a heavy pan over medium heat. Fry the mustard seeds until they pop. Stir in the asafoetida and the remaining half teaspoon of carom seeds.
5. Gently place the spice-coated colocasia pieces in the oil. Cook on a medium-high heat gently shaking the pan at regular intervals. Allow to cook for 3-4 minutes over low heat until you get a golden crust.
6. Remove from the pan and sprinkle dried fenugreek leaves crushed between finger tips. Serve hot with rotis. These can also be served as an appetizer.

- *Colocasia is known to cause bloating and ajwain is one of the best remedies in the kitchen cabinet to combat bloating and gassiness. So these two ingredients make a perfect match in this recipe.*

Hagalakayi Gojju

Bitter Gourd Curry

TIME TAKEN: 50 MINUTES | SERVES 4

Gojju is a spicy, tangy, and sweet preparation from the southern state of Karnataka, typically had with steamed rice and ghee. It is prepared with a variety of vegetables and even fruits like pineapple and grapes. If you are a fan of salty-sweet flavours in a dish, this one is a must try.

Ingredients

3-4 medium sized (225 g) bitter gourds /
  2 cups chopped (karela)
¼ cup (40 g) tamarind + 2 cups water
2 tbsp peanut oil
1 tsp black mustard seeds
1 tsp split skinned urad dal
½ tsp ground turmeric
2 sprigs curry leaves
2 tsp salt
2 tsp rasam powder
2 tsp Kashmiri red chilli powder depends on heat
¼ cup (50 g) crushed jaggery

Method

1. Slice the bitter gourds vertically. Remove seeds and inner white pith and dice it finely.
2. Soak the tamarind in water for 20 minutes. Squeeze the soaked tamarind to extract the pulp. Discard the squeezed tamarind pieces and keep the extract aside.
3. In a pan, heat the oil. Fry mustard seeds until they start popping. Add in the urad dal and fry over medium heat until golden brown in colour.
4. To this, combine the chopped bitter gourd and fry over low to medium heat for 15 minutes. This will change colour to a duller green and the bitter gourd gets partially cooked. Sprinkle turmeric and stir in curry leaves. Stir well to combine and cook for another 5 minutes.
5. At this point, pour the tamarind extract along with ½ cup of boiling hot water and let it come to a simmer over high heat. Allow to boil for 5-7 minutes and the tamarind extract to thicken. Add salt, rasam powder, chilli powder, and powdered jaggery. Allow the 'gojju' to boil for another 2-3 minutes. The consistency of the gojju is much thicker than dal so make sure you don't add too much water.
6. You can try the same recipe using sliced okra or green grapes.

- *The colour of the gojju depends on the tamarind used. A darker aged variety of tamarind will give a dark brown gojju.*
- *Acidity varies depending on tamarind, so taste as you go to balance chilli, jaggery, and salt.*
- *1 tbsp coarsely powdered white sesame seeds can be added in the final stage.*

Cholar Dal

Bengali-style Gram Dal

PREP TIME: 2 HOURS;
COOKING TIME: 20 MINUTES | SERVES 4-6

Of all the lentils used in Indian cuisine, chana dal has the most complex flavour and unmistakable texture. Sliced coconut and raisins add a unique flavour to this Bengali staple.

Ingredients

1 cup (180 g) Bengal gram (chana dal)

2 tsp salt, divided

3 bay leaves, divided

2" piece (25 g) ginger, thinly sliced

2 tsp ground coriander

1 tsp ground cumin

½ tsp ground turmeric

2 tbsp mustard oil*

3 tbsp thinly sliced fresh coconut**

2-3 dried red chillies

3 green cardamoms

2 1" cinnamon sticks

1 tsp cumin seeds

¼ tsp asafoetida

3-4 green chillies, slit

2 tbsp raisins

2 tsp sugar

½ tsp garam masala powder

Method

1. Soak the chana dal in plenty of water for 2 hours. Drain and place in a pressure cooker with 2½ cups of water. Add 2 bay leaves and 1 teaspoon salt. Pressure cook for one whistle (full pressure) and then on lowest heat (sim) for 5-7 minutes. The dal should be cooked. Note that the dal should retain its shape and not be cooked to a mush. You can also cook it on the stove top. This may take around 30 minutes.

2. In a small mixer jar or a spice grinder, blend the ginger, ground coriander, ground cumin and ground turmeric with 1-2 tbsp of water to get a fine paste. Keep this aside.

3. Heat the mustard oil in a deep pan. Fry the coconut slices until golden brown. Remove with a slotted spoon. Set aside.

4. In the same oil, fry the dried red chillies, 1 bay leaf, green cardamom, cinnamon, and cumin seeds for a few seconds until the spices bloom. Stir in the asafoetida.

5. Add the prepared ginger-spice paste to this and cook for 3-4 minutes over medium heat. Combine the slit green chillies and fry for 30 seconds.

6. Transfer the cooked dal into the pan, reserving some of the clear water to be added later depending on the consistency. Add the remaining 1 teaspoon salt, sugar, raisins and garam masala powder and allow the dal to simmer for 3-4 minutes. It should have a thick consistency. If the dal is too thick, add some of the reserved dal water and simmer for 2 minutes or so.

7. Add the fried coconut slices in the last stage of simmering. Serve hot with rice, pulao, luchi, or motorshuti kochuri (page 160).

*   *Mustard oil lends Bengali dishes its characteristic flavour. In its absence, you can substitute it for a neutral flavoured oil.*
** *The coconut should be unsweetened. Do not use grated coconut.*

Pao Bhaji

Mixed Vegetable Mash with Bread

COOKING TIME: 50 MINUTES | SERVES 4-6

This popular Mumbai street food is best served with soft buttered pan-toasted pav and a blob of butter melting into the hot vegetable mix.

Ingredients

4-6 dried red chillies (Kashmiri or byadagi)

6 cloves garlic

2 tsp oil

1 tsp pav bhaji masala

3 medium sized (350 g) potatoes, peeled and chopped

1 large (100 g) carrot, peeled and diced

1 small (30 g) beet, peeled and diced

½ cup (60 g) green peas, fresh or frozen

1 cup (100 g) cauliflower florets (optional)

6 medium-sized (400 g) tomatoes, chopped

1 tsp salt

1 tbsp oil

1 tbsp butter

1 large onion, finely diced / 1½ cups finely chopped

1 large capsicum (green bell pepper), deseeded and finely diced

1 tbsp pav bhaji masala

1 tsp kasuri methi (optional)

2-3 tbsp finely chopped fresh coriander

Salt to taste

8 pieces pav (dinner rolls)

Salted butter

TO SERVE ON THE SIDE

Lime wedges

Finely chopped onions

Fresh coriander leaves, chopped

Method

1. Soak the chillies and garlic in a bowl of hot water for half an hour. Drain and grind to a fine paste. Keep aside.

2. In a pressure cooker, heat 2 teaspoon oil. Stir in the pav bhaji masala and salt. Add the prepped vegetables and sauté for 1-2 minutes over high heat. Add 1 cup water and bring to a simmer. Close the cooker lid and pressure cook for 5-6 minutes.

3. Meanwhile, in a large pan, heat the oil and butter. Add the chopped onions and capsicum. Sauté for 10 minutes over low-medium heat. To this, add the prepared chilli-garlic paste, pav bhaji masala (1 tbsp), kasuri methi, and coriander leaves. Fry this over medium heat for another 5-7 minutes to cook out the chilli-garlic paste.

4. Open the cooker once the pressure has released. Using a masher or the back of a ladle or a hand blender, coarse crush the cooked vegetables. Add this to the pan along with the liquids. Check for salt and adjust. Simmer for 8-10 minutes while mashing the mixture off and on, adding more hot water if required for a pourable consistency. The mixture will sputter while simmering. You may cover it partially with a lid to avoid too much of a mess.

5. To prepare the pav, slice it horizontally, apply some butter on the inside and outside and spread it out on a hot tava or skillet until golden brown spots appear.

6. Serve hot pav with a bowl of bhaji topped with some more butter and the fresh garnishes like lime, onion, and coriander on the side.

Thenga Saadham

Coconut Rice

TIME TAKEN: 30 MINUTES | SERVES 6

The crunchy tempering made up of lentils and the cashew nuts add delicious textures to the dish.

Ingredients

1½ cups (300 g) short grain rice like
   jeeraga samba
1 tsp salt
2 tbsp coconut oil
½ tsp mustard seeds
1 tbsp skinned black lentils (urad dal)
1 tbsp Bengal gram (chana dal)
2-3 dried red chillies
2 tbsp cashew halves
¾ cup fresh grated coconut

Method

1. Wash and drain the rice 2-3 times. Pressure cook the rice with 3 cups water and ¾ tsp salt for 1 whistle and then on low heat for 5 minutes. Alternatively, cook the rice using the rice cooker or the stove top method. Remove to a large dish and separate out the grains. Allow to cool.
2. In a large, heavy-bottomed pan, heat the oil. Add the mustard seeds. Once the seeds splutter, add the urad dal and chana dal. Fry until golden brown.
3. Add the dried red chillies and cashew nuts. Fry until the cashews are golden brown. Stir in the grated coconut with the remaining ¼ teaspoon of salt.
4. Mix the rice and gently combine all the ingredients. The flavours of the coconut and fried dals infuse into the rice better if kept aside for an hour or so.

Vari Cha Chawal

Barnyard Millet 'Rice'

TIME TAKEN: 15 MINUTES | SERVES 3

Barnyard millet goes by many names in India – vari, samo, samak, bhagar, vrat ke chawal, samvat, to list a few. In many communities in India, cereals are not eaten during fasts. Pseudograins like vari are therefore eaten instead of rice or prepared into other dishes.

Ingredients

1 cup (200 g) barnyard millet (bhagar)
2 tsp ghee
½ tsp cumin seeds
1-2 green chillies
¾ tsp salt

Method

1. Rinse the barnyard millet in water and drain.
2. Heat the ghee in a pan over medium heat. Fry the cumin seeds and green chillies for a few seconds. Add the millet and fry for 3-4 minutes. Add 2 cups of water. Season with salt.
3. Bring the mixture to a boil and then reduce the heat. Cover and cook for 8-10 minutes until the grains are cooked.
4. Uncover and fluff up with a fork. Serve immediately with shengdanyachi amti.

- *Cooked barnyard millet can be used as a gluten-free binder to make croquettes or patties with a mix of vegetables and beans.*

Fangavela Mug

Sprouted Mung Bean Dry Curry

COOKING TIME: 15 MINUTES | SERVES 4

This austere Gujarati dish made with sprouted whole moong beans is the usual accompaniment to kadhi (a yoghurt based spicy curry) and rice. The technique of stove top cooking allows you to have an al dente texture to the cooked dish rather than mushy and overcooked. This dry moong sprout preparation is a great addition to a Buddha bowl or in a sandwich stuffing. You can either soak and sprout the moong beans over 2-4 days (depending on the weather) or buy ready sprouts.

Ingredients

1½ cups whole green moong or 4-5 cups
   of sprouts
1 large (200 g) onion
1 tbsp oil
1 tsp cumin seeds
Pinch of asafoetida
2-3 green chillies, slit vertically
1 sprig curry leaves
½ tsp ground turmeric
1 tbsp ground coriander
Salt, to taste

GARNISH
2 tbsp fresh grated coconut
2 tbsp chopped fresh coriander leaves
Lime juice as needed

Method

1. If using whole moong beans, soak them in plenty of water overnight. Drain the water the following morning and follow your favoured method of sprouting to get half an inch long sprouts. If buying ready sprouts, wash in clean water, drain, and keep aside.
2. Peel, halve and slice the onion thinly.
3. Heat the oil in a pan with a fitting lid. Fry cumin seeds. Once they sizzle, add asafoetida, green chillies, and curry leaves. Sauté for a few seconds.
4. Transfer the sprouts to the pan along with turmeric and ground coriander. Season with salt.
5. Sauté over high heat for 30 seconds. Add 1 cup water to the pan and cover with the lid.
6. Reduce the heat to medium. It will take around 8 minutes for the sprouts to be cooked while retaining a bite.
7. Dry out any excess water in the pan. Remove to a boil and garnish with coconut, coriander, and lime juice.
8. Serve with rice and kadhi or with phulka/rotis.

- *If buying ready sprouts, do note that the Asian style bean sprouts won't work well in this recipe. There needs to be a substantial bean component too.*
- *The same recipe works well for sprouted moth beans, called matki in some Indian languages.*

Kollu Rasam

Horse Gram Soup

PREP TIME: 8 HOURS;
COOKING TIME: 30 MINUTES | SERVES 4

Horse gram has a thick outer skin, therefore, it is ideal to soak it overnight or for 10 hours minimum. The rasam uses the cooking water along with some of the cooked gram, while the rest can be used to make a salad-like dish with a tempering, called sundal.

Ingredients

½ cup horse gram, soaked overnight
2 tbsp tamarind flakes
1 medium-sized tomato
1½ tsp rock salt
½ tsp ground turmeric
2-3 cloves garlic, peeled
1 tbsp chopped fresh coriander

FOR RASAM POWDER
1 tsp black peppercorns
2 tsp cumin seeds
1 tbsp coriander seeds
1-2 dried red chillies

TEMPERING
1 tbsp ghee
½ tsp cumin seeds
1 sprig curry leaves
Pinch of asafoetida

Method

1. Drain the soaking water and place the horse gram in a pressure cooker. Add 2 cups of water and pressure cook for 15-20 minutes (i.e. after one whistle or full pressure, reduce the heat to low and cook for 15-20 minutes). When the pressure recedes, open the cooker. Separate the cooking liquid and the beans. Don't discard the cooking liquid as this is the body of the rasam. Mash the cooked beans in a food processor or a potato masher to get a coarse puree.

2. Soak the tamarind in 1 cup of hot water for 30 minutes. Squeeze out all the tamarind extract using your fingers and discard the tamarind solids. Add the tamarind extract to a pot.

3. Chop and grind the tomato to a puree. Mix it with the tamarind extract. Add 1 cup of water to this. Season this liquid with salt and turmeric. Crush the garlic cloves and add it to the pot. Bring this to a simmer to cook off the raw smell of tamarind. This should take around 5-7 minutes of boiling.

4. In a small pan over medium heat, dry roast the spices for the rasam powder. Grind it to a coarse powder in a small mixer jar. Keep the heat on the lowest setting. Combine the horse gram cooking liquid, crushed cooked horse gram, and the fresh spice powder. Add some hot water to bring the rasam to a thin soup like consistency. Let this come to a gentle simmer. Once you see frothing on the surface of the pot, turn off the heat.

5. In the same small pan, heat the ghee. Add the cumin seeds and curry leaves. Once the cumin sizzles, add asafoetida and give it a quick stir. Transfer over the rasam. Garnish with fresh coriander and keep covered until ready to serve with rice.

Sweets

Sitaphal Kheer

Custard Apple Milk Pudding

TIME TAKEN: 1 HOUR | SERVES 4-6

Sitaphal or custard apple lives up to its English name. The sweet flesh of a ripe fruit with the texture of custard, while it can be relished on its own, it finds its way to quite a few Indian desserts, like this pudding or kheer. The fruit does have a rather annoying seed to pulp ratio and separating the pulp is an exercise in patience, but it is well rewarded in a seasonal dessert like this one.

Ingredients

1 litre full cream milk
½ cup (100 g) sugar
½ tsp green cardamom powder
2 large (500 g) ripe custard apples

GARNISH
2-3 tsp pistachio slivers

Method

1. Take the milk in a heavy-bottomed pan for stove top cooking. This needs constant monitoring and stirring for at least 45 minutes until the milk has reduced by a third, after which you may add the sugar and let it simmer for another 10-15 minutes.
2. It is much easier and hands-free to make it in an electronic pressure cooker. Add the milk and sugar into the container. Use the Pressure Cook setting, selecting High Pressure for 40 minutes. Once the pressure lowers, open the cooker. The milk will be well thickened.
3. Stir in the cardamom powder.
4. Remove the pulp of the custard apples and discard the seeds and peels.
5. Add ¾th of the pulp to the kheer and stir gently. Let it cool a bit after which it needs to be refrigerated for 3-4 hours. Divide the kheer between 4-6 cups and garnish with the remaining pulp and a few slivers of pistachios.

Pachapayaru Vella Sundal

Sweet Green Moong

TIME TAKEN: 4 HOURS 25 MINUTES, INCLUDING SOAKING TIME | SERVES 4-6

Soaked green moong cooks quickly and it can be made into this minimalist sweet preparation that is offered to the gods during festivals in South India. You can also try a savoury version.*

Ingredients

1 cup (200 g) whole green moong (soaked for 4-6 hours)
Pinch of salt
1 tbsp ghee
½ cup (75 g) powdered jaggery
½ cup (50 g) grated coconut (fresh, unsweetened)
½ tsp green cardamom powder**

Method

1. Drain the soaked green moong. Cook it in either a pan of water on the stove top with a pinch of salt until soft (5-6 minutes) or in a pressure cooker (turn off at full pressure/one whistle). Moong should be well cooked but maintaining its shape and not turning mushy. Drain the moong. The water can be used in other dals or soups.
2. Heat ghee in a pan. Add the drained cooked moong to this along with jaggery and coconut.
3. Reduce the heat to low and stir to combine for 4-5 minutes. Add cardamom powder towards the end and combine well.
4. Transfer to a bowl and garnish with some more fresh coconut.

* For a savoury version, cook green moong similarly. Heat 1 tbsp coconut oil in a pan. Add mustard and cumin seeds. Once mustard splutters, add sliced green chillies, and curry leaves and fry for a minute. Add the drained moong, salt, turmeric, lime juice, and coconut. Makes for an excellent side dish or a salad.

** Remove the seeds of 2-3 green cardamoms and crush in a mortar pestle with a pinch of granulated sugar to get a coarse powder.

Ragi Laddoo
Finger Millet Sweet

TIME TAKEN: 30 MINUTES | MAKES 15

Ancient Indian energy balls made using nutrient rich finger millets and unprocessed sugar with the goodness and flavour of homemade ghee, satisfies a post-meal sweet-tooth craving or something to fuel a trek or a run too.

Ingredients

1 cup (125 g) ragi flour
¾ cup (100 g) raw cane sugar (khandsari)
3 tbsp ghee
2 tbsp cashew nuts (piece)
1 tsp ground ginger (sonth)
4-5 tbsp milk

Method

1. Roast ragi flour in a pan for 8-10 minutes until aromatic. Do not let it turn brown.
2. Grind the raw cane sugar to a powder.
3. Add this to the ragi flour in a large bowl.
4. Heat the ghee in a pan and fry cashew pieces until they turn golden brown.
5. Transfer the ghee to the bowl and with firm hands try and bring it together to a rough dough.
6. In the final stage add milk, a tablespoon at a time and continue kneading.
7. Once it comes together to form a dough, don't add any more milk.
8. Divide into 15 pieces or 20 gram portions. With a firm hand press it together and roll into a ball.
9. Variation: 2 tablespoons of the thandai mix can be added to the ragi mixture and then make into laddoos for spicy tones.

WinteR

Given India's great geographic and climatic diversity, only a few states close to the Himalayas or at higher altitudes, experience a full-blown winter with freezing temperatures. In some parts, the weather turns pleasant, and in the plains, it is business as usual, with just a slight relief from the heat. An abundance of fresh, seasonal produce combined with a series of festivals are some of the reasons why winters are the best time of the year in most parts of India.

Winters in Kashmir

'Find the invincible summer in your heart when you, in the depths of winter, come to the slopes of the Vale where even gods have sought refuge... and then regard the frost and the pines crusted with snow,' writes poet Agha Shahid Ali about winters in Kashmir, hailed as paradise on earth.

Kashmir, the northernmost region of India, experiences the most noteworthy of winters in the country. Nearly landlocked for three months during winter, the Kashmiri language has terms to describe various degrees of winter during the season. The harshest winter starting from the winter solstice on 21 December and lasting forty days is called *chillai kalan* (major cold). This is the period when maximum snowfall is expected. People stock up on essentials as in many instances, villages and towns get cut off due to snow blocking roads or electricity outages. This is followed by twenty days of *chillai khurd* (small cold), and then ten days of *chillai bachcha* (baby cold) ending around early March.

Because of the inclement weather, winter cuisine in Kashmir makes use of sun-dried vegetables called hokh syun. Bottle gourd, eggplant, apples, turnip, tomatoes, and even fish, are dried in June and July. Greens like hakh (collard greens), dandelion, methi, spinach and mushrooms are also sun dried and cooked in dishes by themselves or combined with meat to make hearty curries.

Cooking seasonal

Rabi crops are sown at the end of monsoon and harvested all through winter, extending up to April. Wheat, barley, peas, gram, and mustard are the main winter harvests. Fenugreek, onions, potatoes, oats are also some of the crops harvested in the winters. For anyone who loves to cook or eat, winter is the best season in India, especially for those living in favourable climatic locations. Vegetables like carrots, green peas, cauliflower, broccoli, turnip and radish are at their best during winters. Green leafy vegetables are plenty in stock and stay fresh for longer.

In Punjab, sarson ka saag (mustard greens mash) with makke di roti (corn rotis) served with jaggery and freshly churned white butter deserves all the adulation it gets. Even when served at a simple roadside dhaba, this makes for an unforgettable meal. Whole sweet potatoes with skins roasted over coals is a street delicacy that is looked forward to in the northern parts of India in winters.

Winter pickles made with cauliflower, carrot, and turnip is a Punjabi specialty. Fresh green peas are the highlight ingredient of a curry called nimona, popular in Uttar Pradesh. Fresh peas combined with spices to make a paste, forms a filling inside a puri to make koraishutir kochuri.

In the Northeast, stews using seasonal vegetables and greens along with chillies, ginger and edible soda are prepared as a warming meal during the winters, each region having its own tweaks to the stew recipe. It is either had as a soup or served with rice.

In a Gujarati home, if summers are for aamras, winters are for undhiyu, a dry vegetable preparation made using a medley of winter vegetables like beans (surti papdi), green pigeon peas, fenugreek leaves, purple yam, potatoes in spicy coriander, garlic, chilli, and coconut paste. This slow cooked smoky dish is eaten with rotis or puris.

Fresh turmeric root, which is a winter luxury, is julienned and mixed with salt and lime or lemon juice to make an instant pickle that is served with many meals during the season. Mogri, or rat-tailed radish, belongs to the mustard family. Available in both green and purple colours, its pungency can be tamed by sautéed it in a bit of oil and serving it with bajra rotis or by mixing with yoghurt and making a raita.

Black carrots make their appearance in the markets of northern India during peak winters. These are used to make a drink fermented with mustard seeds called kanji. As the wedding season in many parts of India falls during winters, a lot of elaborate wedding menus incorporate the seasonal produce. Pairing seasonal vegetables and produce with warming spices like cinnamon, cardamom, ginger, black pepper and cumin makes for simple, nourishing meals with maximum flavour that provide comfort in the cold months of the year.

Sweets for the winter

Winter desserts in India are aplenty. Featuring ingredients like jaggery, nolen gur, khus khus, alsi (watercress seeds), gond (edible gum), seasonal vegetables and an abashed quantity of ghee, it is good to experience and enjoy these in moderation.

Gaajar ka halwa is the most iconic dessert made using seasonal red carrots cooked along with reduced milk and sugar, garnished with a smattering of nuts.

Daulat ki chaat/ malai makkhan/ Malaiyyo is a famous dessert of Purani Dilli (Old Delhi), a dessert that is typically eaten early in the morning. Thickened milk and cream, it is left out in the cold night air, allowing nature to work its magic. The dew collected overnight foams up the milk and cream, it is then sweetened and sold in earthen pots, melting fully in one's mouth.

Gond pak edible gum cakes are a fascinating ingredient. Fried, crushed and added to laddoos, it brings an unmistakable crunchy and chewy texture to sweets. It is said to be warming and also used in laddoos along with different ingredients depending on the region.

Relax into your evening cooking regime by tuning into a custom evening raagas playlist.

Nolen gur (date palm jaggery) is available only for a short period in the winters in West Bengal. A number of mishti or sweets are made using this ingredient during the season. Sweets like sandesh have a caramel colour from this jaggery. Modern desserts like ice creams are also made using nolen gur.

SCAN ME

Pitha is very popular in eastern India. This are rice flour-based sweets that are either in crepes, fritter or dumpling form usually prepared for Sankranti. These have a stuffing of coconut, jaggery, nuts, dried fruit and flavoured with cardamom or edible camphor, and they can be steamed, fried, or pan fried.

Appetizers, Drinks, Condiments

Shakarkandi Chaat

Street-style Sweet Potatoes

Shakarkandi chaat is sold on street carts in winters in North India. This is made from sweet potatoes roasted on coals stacked in portable stoves. In this chaat, roasted sweet potatoes are seasoned with dry spice powders like chaat masala, red chilli powder, and rock salt along with lime juice, green chillies, and coriander. The green and sweet chutneys along with roasted peanuts brings more flavour, colour, and texture to the chaat.

Ingredients

2 medium sized (250 g) sweet potatoes
2 tsp oil
½ tsp black salt
4 tsp green chutney
2 tsp tamarind sweet chutney
1 tsp chaat masala
½ tsp red chilli powder
2 tsp pomegranate arils
2 tbsp chopped fresh coriander
2 tbsp coarsely crushed roasted peanuts
4 tsp fine sev

Method

1. Scrub and wash the sweet potatoes. Slice into 1 cm thin discs. Grease a flat pan or a tava with some oil. Place the slices in a single layer and cook over medium heat for 3-4 minutes on each side until the sweet potato is cooked and golden brown. Do this in batches until all the slices are cooked. Keep aside.
2. On each plate, arrange 10-12 slices of sweet potato. Sprinkle a pinch of black salt. Drizzle green chutney and tamarind chutney as per your liking. Sprinkle chaat masala, red chilli powder, some pomegranate arils, and chopped coriander over the sweet potato slices.
3. Top with crunchy peanuts and sev. Serve immediately.

• *You can prepare a similar chaat using oven roasted slices of potatoes or just chunks of boiled potato.*

Methi Na Muthia

Fried Dumplings with Fenugreek Leaves

TIME TAKEN: 40 MINUTES | SERVES 6

A winter specialty from Gujarat with the deep flavour of fresh methi leaves, this makes for a delicious tea time snack. These deep fried treats also make excellent travel companions.

Ingredients

2 cups (120 g) chopped fenugreek leaves
½ cup (30 g) chopped fresh coriander
½ tsp salt
¾ cup (100 g) whole wheat flour
¼ cup (40 g) semolina (rava)
¼ cup (30 g) gram flour
2 tbsp sesame seeds
1/8 tsp asafoetida
½ tsp ground turmeric
1 tsp red chilli powder
1 tsp ground coriander
1 tsp ground cumin
1 tbsp grated jaggery or sugar
1 tbsp pickle masala (methia masala)
2 tbsp oil
1 tbsp lime juice
2 cups oil for deep-frying

Method

1. In a large bowl, combine all the ingredients except for the oil for deep-frying.
2. Add water by the spoonful and bind into a firm dough.
3. Divide it into 20 gram portions and roll into a sphere or a cylinder.
4. Heat the oil in a heavy-bottomed frying pan. Once the oil is hot, keep the heat on medium and fry in batches of 6-7 depending on the size of your pan. Do not overcrowd the muthia during the frying process. Turn over after at least 30 seconds of frying so that the muthia doesn't break.
5. Continue frying until dark golden brown on all sides. Remove into a kitchen paper lined sieve. Fry all the batches similarly. Serve as a tea time snack or add it to undhiyu, a mixed vegetable winter preparation from Gujarat.

- *If you cannot find the pickle masala, use 2 tablespoons of oil from a pickle jar and omit the extra oil. In absence of any pickles at home, simply omit the pickle masala and proceed with the recipe.*

Beetroot Kola

Chettinad-style Beetroot Bites

TIME TAKEN: 35 MINUTES | MAKES 16 PIECES

Beetroot with the flavour of a Chettinad curry spices like fennel seeds, cloves, and cinnamon, kola is a delight for the tastebuds. Try these as cocktail starters or even as koftas in your favourite gravy.

Ingredients

2 large (400 g) beetroot
½ tsp ground turmeric
½ tsp red chilli powder
1 tsp salt
¼ cup (15 g) chopped fresh coriander
2 cups oil for deep-frying

FOR SPICE PASTE
1 cup (100 g) grated coconut (frozen is fine)
4 green chillies, broken into half
4 cloves garlic
2 tsp poppy seeds
6 tbsp cashew nut halves
6 tbsp fried gram*
2 green cardamoms
1½" piece cinnamon
4 cloves
1 tsp fennel seeds

Method

1. Peel and grate the beetroot. Squeeze out excess juice (this is not required for the recipe**) and keep the grated beet aside.
2. In a heavy-bottomed pan over medium heat, dry roast all the ingredients for the spice paste for 4-5 minutes, or until the spices are aromatic. None of the ingredients need to be browned. This process is to dry out any excess moisture. Cool this mixture and grind to a coarse paste.
3. In the same pan, dry sauté the grated beetroot for 4-5 minutes over medium heat to remove excess moisture.
4. Add the prepared spice paste, ground turmeric, red chilli powder, salt, and chopped coriander. Continue to stir and combine over low heat until the mixture comes together like a ball of dough. Let this cool.
5. Divide into 16 portions of roughly 25 grams each. Roll each into a smooth ball.
6. Heat the oil in a pan. Once it is hot, deep-fry in batches of 4 until golden brown on the outside. Serve hot along with drinks, as a starter, or along with the main meal.

* *If you cannot find fried gram, use 2-3 tablespoon chickpea flour or use peanuts, or increase the quantity of cashew nuts used.*
** *You can drink up the beetroot juice as is or mixed with some orange juice.*

Motorshutir Kochuri
Deep Fried Flatbreads Stuffed with Fresh Green Peas

TIME TAKEN: 50 MINUTES | MAKES 10

The fresh green peas available in winters makes its way into these kochuris that are invariably a part of Bengali wedding feasts during the season. It is also one of the favourite jolkhabar (a Bengali term for snack) when served with aloor dom (potato curry). A bit of prep the previous night in preparing the dough and the filling makes it a rather easy festive breakfast.

Ingredients

FOR THE DOUGH
1 cup (150 g) all-purpose flour
½ tsp salt
1 tsp sugar
4 tsp cooking oil

FOR THE FILLING
1 cup (150 g) shelled peas (fresh)
3 green chillies
2 tsp finely grated ginger
½ tsp ground cumin
½ tsp salt
1 tsp sugar
2 tsp oil
½ tsp nigella seeds (kalonji)
$1/8$ tsp asafoetida

2 cups oil for deep-frying

Method

1. Combine the ingredients for the dough in a bowl. Make sure the oil is well combined into the dough. Add warm water, a little at a time to make a smooth dough. Cover the bowl and allow it to rest for 15-30 minutes.

2. Meanwhile, prepare the filling. In a saucepan with 2 cups of water, boil the peas for 3-4 minutes until soft. Drain well. Combine with chillies, ginger, cumin powder, salt, and sugar and grind to a fine paste without using any extra water.

3. Heat 2 tsp oil in a pan. Fry the nigella seeds and asafoetida for a few seconds. Scrape the prepared paste into the oil. Stir it over low-medium heat to dry out the moisture. This is to ensure that filling is not soggy. Keep stirring until the mixture comes together into a ball. Remove into a dish and let it cool.

4. Divide the dough and the filling into 10 portions each. Flatten out the dough and make it into a cup in your palm. Add in the filling and cover well and roll into a ball. Using an oiled rolling pin and base, roll out into thick puris 5" diameter size.

5. Heat oil in a wok and deep-fry each such kochuri separately over high heat until it puffs up. Flip it over with a slotted spoon and fry the other side for 20-30 seconds as well.

6. Drain on a kitchen paper to absorb the excess oil.

7. Serve with aloor dom (baby potatoes in Bengali style curry, page 171).

Haldi Ka Achaar

Instant Turmeric Pickle

TIME TAKEN: 15 MINUTES |
MAKES AROUND 150 GRAMS

Instant turmeric pickle is very common in Gujarati households during the winter months. The healing properties of turmeric make it a must have condiment in your thali especially during the winters. Mango ginger, if available can be mixed along with turmeric in this instant pickle.

Ingredients

1¼ cups (150 grams) fresh turmeric root, chopped
3 green chillies
4 limes / lemons
2 tbsp pink Himalayan salt

Method

1. Wash and wipe dry the turmeric roots. Lightly scrape the skins if required. If the roots are clean, then you may avoid scraping the peels.
2. Slice the roots thinly, lengthwise. Pile up slices and chop into 1-inch-long thin juliennes.
3. Slit the green chillies lengthwise.
4. Grate or peel the lime skins using a sharp peeler and chop finely.
5. In a bowl, combine the julienned turmeric, green chillies, chopped lime peel, and salt. Juice the limes into the bowl. Combine all the ingredients with a clean spoon and transfer this into a clean dry glass jar.
6. The instant turmeric pickle can be eaten along with any meal or add a spoonful of this pickle to a salad. The leftover liquid after the pickle is over can be used in the place of lime juice and salt in a salad dressing.

Mooli Ka Thechai

Smashed Radish Condiment

TIME TAKEN: 5 MINUTES | MAKES ½ CUP

Radish is the most delicious winter harvest in the mountains of north India. Crisp and spicy, fresh radish and its leaves are used not just for parathas and salads but also in this very rustic condiment, which is simply ingredients crushed together using stones or in a mortar pestle.

Ingredients

2 small sized (100 g) radishes (mooli)
3-4 green chillies
3 cloves garlic
½ cup (30 g) chopped fresh coriander leaves
Pinch of red chilli powder (optional)
½ tsp rock salt
2 tsp lime juice

Method

1. Peel and dice the radish. Slice the green chillies and garlic.
2. In a large mortar pestle, crush all the ingredients together except lime juice to get a coarse paste. Stir in the lime juice and transfer to a serving bowl.
3. Alternatively, coarsely grate the radish and squeeze out excess water. Grind the remaining ingredients to a coarse paste and mix it well into the grated radish.
4. Serve this thecha as an accompaniment to roti, dal, and vegetables.

Gajar Gobhi Shalgam Achaar

Punjabi Mixed Vegetable Pickle

TIME TAKEN: 1 HR 30 MINUTES |
MAKES 2 BOTTLES ~ 600 GRAMS

Even for an experienced home cook, making pickles can be intimidating. Here are just a few reasons why the process is worthwhile - no chemical preservatives, best quality ingredients, cold pressed oils, and a lower salt content compared to commercial brands.

Ingredients

½ medium-sized (250 g) cauliflower broken into small florets
1 large (150 g) carrot, peeled and diced
1 large (150 g) turnip, peeled and diced
Total quantity of chopped vegetables used for this pickle is 500 grams, roughly 4½ cups
1 tsp salt
50 g ginger, julienned
50 g green chillies, cut into 2-3 pieces each
2 tsp fenugreek seeds
1 tsp fennel seeds
1 tsp black pepper
1 tsp cumin seeds
½ cup (120 ml) mustard oil
2 tbsp ground mustard seeds
1 tsp ground turmeric
¼ tsp asafoetida
1 tsp red chilli powder
1½ tsp salt
¹⁄₆ cup (40 ml) vinegar

Method

1. Place 1 litre of water in a saucepan with a teaspoon of salt over medium heat. Bring to a boil. Add the chopped vegetables to the boiling water. Cover and simmer for 3-4 minutes. Drain using a colander. Let the vegetables sit in the colander for 5 minutes so that the excess water is drained.

2. Keep a large absorbent cotton cloth spread out on a large surface (preferably under a fan). Spread the drained vegetables on the cloth and allow to air dry for 1 hour so that the excess moisture is dried out.

3. Next, prepare the spice mix for the pickle. Heat a small pan. Dry roast fenugreek seeds, fennel seeds, black pepper and cumin over low to medium heat for 2-3 minutes. This is to remove any excess moisture and not to brown the spices. Remove to a plate to cool.

4. Heat the mustard oil in a pan until smoking hot. Remove to a bowl to cool. Add the freshly prepared mixed spice powder to the cooled mustard oil. Also mix in the ground mustard seeds, asafoetida, and ground turmeric.

5. In a large mixing bowl, add the blanched and dried vegetables, chopped ginger and chillies, mustard oil with spices, red chilli powder, and salt. Mix well. Pour in the vinegar.

6. Combine gently until the spices coat the vegetables well. The pickle is ready to be eaten but it tastes better after 3-4 days. Store in a clean, dry jar. Refrigerate.

- *You can use any mix of chopped vegetables as long as the quantity remains 500 grams so that the proportion of spices is well balanced. The washed and chopped vegetables can also be sun dried after blanching until the moisture dries out.*

Main Course

Alu Gobhi

Dry Curry with Cauliflower and Potatoes

PREP TIME: 30 MINUTES; COOKING TIME: 20 MINUTES | SERVES 4

A version of this dry curry with cauliflower and potatoes is made in almost all North Indian states. Although it is called alu gobhi, the proportion of cauliflower is more in this ever so popular curry. Deep-frying the veggies until they get a caramelized exterior definitely adds a lot more flavour, but this pan sautéed version is not bad at all, especially if you are not a fan of deep-frying. Fresh green peas that are in season in the winter can also be added to this subzi and so can fresh methi leaves (fenugreek).

Ingredients

1 medium (350 g) cauliflower, broken into florets
1 tsp + 1 tsp salt
2 medium-sized potatoes
2-3 tbsp mustard oil
1 tsp cumin seeds
1½" piece ginger
10 cloves garlic
1-2 green chillies
1 cup (115 g) sliced onions
½ tsp turmeric
1 tsp red chilli powder
1 tbsp coriander powder
2 tsp amchoor powder
½ tsp garam masala powder
3 tbsp chopped fresh coriander

Method

1. Soak the cauliflower florets in a bowl of water with 1 tsp salt for 15-20 minutes. Wash a couple of times, drain and keep aside.
2. Peel and dice the potatoes into 8 pieces each.
3. Crush the ginger, garlic, and green chilli to a paste using spice grinder or mortar pestle. Alternately, use 1½ tablespoon ginger-garlic paste and finely mince the green chillies.
4. Heat the oil in a large heavy-bottomed pan until smoking. Reduce heat and add cumin seeds. Fry for a few seconds.
5. Add the chopped onions and fry over medium heat for 6-7 minutes or until they turn a shade of light brown.
6. Add the prepared ginger-garlic-chilli paste and stir well to combine. Cook this for another 6-7 minutes until the raw smell of garlic is mellowed.
7. To this, add the salt, turmeric, red chilli powder, coriander powder, amchoor powder and fry over low heat until the oil separates.
8. To this spice mix in the pan, add the prepared cauliflower and potatoes and toss well to coat with the masalas.
9. Keep the heat low and the pan covered with a tight lid. Allow this to steam cook for 10-15 minutes. Open the lid every 3-4 minutes to give it a stir.
10. Once the vegetables are cooked, sprinkle garam masala and fresh coriander and toss gently to combine.
11. Serve hot with rotis or dal and rice.

Monje Haakh

Kashmiri Kohlrabi Stew

TIME TAKEN: 20 MINUTES | SERVES 4

Kohlrabi is one of the favourite vegetables among Kashmiris. It is cooked in dozens of different dishes, from pickles to combining it with fish and even tripe. This simple stew can be prepared in minutes in the pressure cooker and enjoyed with plain rice.

Ingredients

4 medium sized (300 g) kohlrabi with leaves
2 tbsp mustard oil
Generous pinch of asafoetida
2 green chillies, halved
1-2 dried red chillies
½ tsp salt
Pinch of baking soda

Method

1. Choose tender kohlrabi for the recipe with fresh leaves. Peel the skin of the kohlrabis, cut into halves and each half into half inch thick slices. Roughly chop the leaves.
2. In a pressure cooker, heat the mustard oil until smoking hot. Turn off the heat and stir in the asafoetida so that it does not burn. Restart the heat and add in the chopped kohlrabi pieces. Sauté for 3-4 minutes after which you can add in the chopped leaves. Sauté for 2-3 minutes until the leaves are wilted.
3. Stir in the chillies, salt, and 1 cup of water. Sprinkle baking soda and give it a stir. Close the lid of the cooker with the weight on and allow it to come to full pressure (first whistle). Reduce heat and cook for 6 minutes. Release the pressure by lifting the weight with a ladle and open the lid so that the greens retain their colour. Serve hot with rice.
4. Monje haakh is flavoured with a bit of Kashmiri ver masala in the end, but if you don't have that, it is fine even without it.

Rajma

Kidney Beans Curry

Rajma-chawal is a popular Sunday lunch menu in North India. Families have their own way of cooking it and their own favourite accompaniments.

Ingredients

1 cup (250 g) Jammu rajma
¼ cup (60 g) mustard oil*
2 large (250 g) onions, thinly sliced
4 medium sized (350 g) tomatoes,
   roughly chopped
1½ tbsp ginger-garlic paste
½ tsp ground turmeric
1 tbsp ground coriander
1 tbsp Kashmiri red chilli powder
2 tsp salt
2 tsp kasuri methi
2 tbsp finely chopped fresh coriander

Method

1. Wash and soak the kidney beans overnight or for 8 hours. Drain, rinse, and place in a pressure cooker with enough water to cover the beans. Cook over high heat until one whistle. Reduce the heat to minimum (sim) and continue cooking for 15 minutes. Remove from the heat and allow the pressure to release naturally.

2. Heat mustard oil in a deep, heavy-bottomed pan until smoking hot. Add the sliced onions and fry over medium heat until well browned. Remove with a slotted spoon to a dish. Once cooled, grind to a paste in a mixer jar and keep aside.

3. Take the roughly chopped tomatoes in a blender or mixer and make a fine puree. Keep aside.

4. In the same oil, fry the ginger-garlic paste over low heat for 2-3 minutes until the raw smell is gone. To this, add the ground turmeric, tomato puree, and the rest of the ground spices.

5. Fry for 5-6 minutes until the puree is reduced and the oil starts appearing on the sides.

6. Stir in the prepared fried onion paste and salt. Fry for 1-2 minutes until well combined.

7. Add the cooked rajma along with the cooking water. Cover and simmer for 5-7 minutes, adding some hot water if required to adjust the consistency.

8. Garnish with crushed kasuri methi and fresh coriander and serve hot with steamed rice.

* If mustard oil is not available, use any other vegetable oil or ghee.
• Fried onions give a complex sweet flavour, but it also takes extra oil and cooking time. Instead of using the fried onion paste, start with 1-2 tablespoons of oil (instead of 4 tablespoons), fry the ginger-garlic paste and then add finely chopped onions to sauté until brown. Add in tomato puree next and proceed as per the recipe above.

Dum Aloo/Aloor Dom

Bengali Style Potatoes in a Curry

TIME TAKEN: 45 MINUTES | SERVES 4

The Bengali preparation of dum aloo is typically made with small new potatoes that are harvested in the winter. The dish is also called 'niramish dum aloo' as it is made without onion and garlic, and is considered suitable for offerings in religious worship. Dum aloo or aloor dom is served along with luchi or kochuri for a relaxed holiday breakfast.

Ingredients

500 g baby potatoes
1½ tsp salt
3 tbsp mustard oil
1 bay leaf
2 pieces (1") cinnamon
4-6 cloves
2 green cardamoms
1 tsp cumin seeds
1 tbsp ginger paste (page 33)
½ tsp ground turmeric
¼ cup (55 g) tomato puree
1 tsp salt
2 tsp sugar
¼ cup (60 g) thick yoghurt
1 tbsp ground coriander
1 tsp ground cumin
2 tsp Kashmiri red chilli powder
½ tsp garam masala powder

Method

1. Boil the baby potatoes in salted water for 20-25 minutes until tender. Peel and keep aside.
2. In a heavy bottomed pan, heat mustard oil until smoking. Add the bay leaf, cinnamon, cloves, cardamom, and cumin seeds. Fry for a few seconds until the spices are aromatic.
3. Add the ginger paste to the spices. Stir constantly for 1-2 minutes so that it does not stick to the pan.
4. Add turmeric, tomato puree, salt, and sugar. Simmer over medium heat for 3-4 minutes until the oil starts separating.
5. Meanwhile, add ground coriander, cumin, and red chilli powder to the yoghurt. Whisk well and ensure there are no lumps.
6. Reduce the heat and add the yoghurt mix to the spice/tomato mixture in the pan. Stir constantly. Cook for 2-3 minutes.
7. Add the baby potatoes. Toss well to coat with the spices. Pour 2 cups of hot water into the pan. Cover and simmer over low heat for 10 minutes so that the potatoes absorb all the flavours.
8. Serve hot with puris or kochuri (page 160).

- If you cannot find baby potatoes or small sized potatoes, use regular sized ones cut into quarters.
- Traditionally, the boiled and peeled potatoes are deep fried before adding to the curry. I have found that skipping that step doesn't alter the end result much.

Sarson Ka Saag

Mustard Greens Mash

COOKING TIME: 50 MINUTES | SERVES 4

This much loved specialty from Punjab is a meal to relish in the winter when the mustard greens are in season. Best had with hand-patted corn meal rotis (makki ki roti).

Ingredients

6-7 cups (400 g) finely chopped mustard greens (sarson saag) (leaves only)
2 cups (200 g) finely chopped spinach
1 cup (40 g) chopped coriander
1 green chilli
6 cloves garlic, chopped
1 tsp grated ginger
1 tsp salt
2 tbsp corn meal (makai atta)

FOR TADKA
2 tbsp ghee
8 cloves garlic, chopped
2 large onions (1 cup, finely chopped)

TO FINISH
1-2 tbsp white unsalted butter

Method

1. In a pressure cooker, combine the chopped mustard greens, spinach, and coriander along with chilli, grated ginger, chopped garlic, and 1 teaspoon salt. Add 1 cup water. Pressure cook for 1 whistle (full pressure) and reduce the heat to cook for 25-30 minutes. The mustard greens take time to break down, which is why the longer cooking time.
2. Meanwhile, prepare the tadka (tempering). In a pan, heat 2 tablespoons ghee. Fry the chopped garlic and finely chopped onions over medium heat for 8-10 minutes until the onions turn golden brown and soft.
3. Open the cooker when the pressure has released. Reduce the heat to low. Mix in the corn meal by the spoonful and keep stirring so it gets absorbed into the greens mash and thickens the residual liquid. Once all of the corn meal is mixed well, allow the mixture to simmer for another 5-7 minutes so that the corn meal is cooked.
4. Transfer the prepared tadka over the greens mash and combine well.
5. Add butter to finish the saag. Serve hot with makki ki rotis (corn meal rotis) or any bread of your choice.

- *If you cannot source mustard greens, use 2-3 different kinds of green leafy vegetables to prepare a similar dish. Radish greens are a good substitute.*

Sindhi Sai Bhaji

Mixed Vegetables, Greens and Lentils

TIME TAKEN: 3 HRS 30 MINUTES,
INCLUDING SOAKING TIME | SERVES 4-6

Sai bhaji is one of the most well-known dishes in Sindhi cuisine. A one pot curry made using lentils, greens, and seasonal vegetables, it is simple and wholesome. All you need is some rice and you have a hearty vegetarian meal ready. The list of ingredients may seem long, but these are all everyday foods that you will find easily in your kitchen. It is a great choice for a potluck dish as you can quickly prepare a large pot of this curry with minimal effort.

Ingredients

1 cup (180 g) Bengal gram (chana dal)
1 small (50 g) sweet potato
1 small (50 g) brinjal
3 cups (300 g) finely chopped spinach
1 cup (20 g) loosely packed dill
1 cup (50 g) chopped methi
3 small (50 g) colocasia root, peeled
½ cup (50 g) chopped green beans

FOR TADKA 1
2 tbsp ghee
Pinch of asafoetida
1 tsp cumin seeds
1 tbsp ginger-garlic paste
1 large onion, chopped
3 large tomatoes, chopped
1 tsp salt
1 tbsp ground coriander
1 tsp red chilli powder
½ tsp ground turmeric

FOR TADKA 2
1 tbsp ghee
6 cloves garlic, finely chopped

Method

1. Soak chana dal in water for 2-3 hours. Drain and keep aside.
2. Peel and chop the sweet potato into a 1" dice. Slice off the crown of the brinjal and chop similarly.
3. In a pressure cooker, combine the drained dal, chopped greens, and chopped vegetables. Pour 3 cups of water. Close the lid and put the weight on. Pressure cook over high heat for 1 whistle (full pressure) and then keep on lowest heat setting for 15 minutes.
4. Open the cooker when the pressure releases and coarsely mash the contents with the back of a ladle.
5. While the dal is cooking, prepare the first tadka.
6. Heat the ghee in a pan over medium heat. Add the asafoetida and fry for a few seconds. Add the cumin seeds.
7. After a few seconds, add the ginger-garlic paste and onions. Fry over medium heat for 7-8 minutes until the onions are golden brown and cooked.
8. Add the tomatoes and salt. Cook until tomatoes are pulpy.
9. Add the ground coriander, red chilli powder and turmeric. Keep stirring to combine well. Transfer this mixture into the mashed dal in the cooker and bring to a simmer.
10. Add around ¼ – ½ cup of hot water to adjust the consistency. Simmer for 5 minutes. Transfer to a serving bowl.
11. In a small pan, prepare the final tadka. Heat the ghee and fry the finely chopped garlic cloves for a minute until they turn golden. Transfer this over the saibhaji in the serving bowl. Serve hot with steamed rice or Sindhi bhuga chawal (page 179).

Pesarattu

Whole Green Moong Crepes

PREP TIME: 6-8 HOURS; COOKING TIME: 20 MINUTES | MAKES 6

An easy breakfast or light meal made using whole green moong beans, this is a staple in the delta regions of the state of Andhra Pradesh. Served with ginger chutney, it sometimes comes with a filling of sautéed onions or with a ladle of upma sandwiched between two halves.

Ingredients

1 cup (200 gram) green moong
3 tbsp rice flour
1-2 green chillies
1" piece ginger
1 tsp salt
2-3 tbsp cooking oil

Method

1. Wash and soak the green moong overnight for 6-8 hours.
2. Drain the moong and transfer to a blender or mixer jar. Add in rice flour, green chillies, ginger, and salt. Grind to a fine puree with the addition of upto 3-4 tablespoons of water. The pesarattu batter is ready. This needs no fermentation and can be used to prepare pesarattu right away.
3. Grease a flat cast iron or non-stick skillet with a few drops of oil.
4. Pour 1-2 ladles (around ¼ cup) of batter in the centre of the hot skillet and make quick concentric circles to spread out the batter in a thin layer. Drizzle a teaspoon of oil around the circumference and let it cook for around a minute over medium heat. Flip over to the other side and use another teaspoon of oil, cook for another 30 seconds and remove to a plate. Repeat the same process with the remaining batter.
5. Serve with tomato thokku (page 86) or any other chutney.

Yellu Saadham

Sesame Rice

TIME TAKEN: 15 MINUTES | SERVES 2-4

Sesame rice with the complex nutty flavour of toasted sesame seeds and skinned black lentils is a unique South Indian dish.

Ingredients

2 cups (400 g) cooked rice (cooked with
   ½ tsp salt)
½ tsp oil
3 dried red chillies
2 tsp dehusked and split black gram (urad dal)
2 tbsp white sesame seeds
½ tsp salt

FOR TEMPERING
1 tbsp gingelly oil
2 dried red chillies
½ tsp mustard seeds
2 tsp dehusked and split black gram (urad dal)
1 sprig curry leaves

Method

1. Ensure that the cooked rice is fluffy and the grains are not sticking to each other. Heat half teaspoon of oil in a small pan. Fry the red chillies and urad dal until the dal is golden. Remove and keep aside. In the same pan, toast the sesame seeds for 4-5 minutes over low heat until it starts popping.
2. Once the popping stops, remove it along with the fried chillies and urad dal into a mixer jar or spice grinder. Grind to a coarse powder along with half teaspoon of salt.
3. Sprinkle the prepared spice mix on the cooked rice. Using fingers or a fork, combine gently to ensure the rice is well coated with the spice mix.
4. In the same pan, heat the oil for tempering. Add the dried red chillies, mustard seeds, urad dal, and curry leaves. Once the mustard seeds pop and dal is golden, pour over the rice.
5. Serve hot along with raita or any vegetable curry.

Sindhi Bhuga Chawal

Sindhi Pulao

PREP TIME: 30 MINUTES; COOKING TIME: 20 MINUTES I SERVES 2-4

Rich with the flavour of browned onions, this easy rice dish is the best accompaniment to Sindhi curries like saibhaji. The colour in this rice is all from the browned onions, so take your time with the process.

Ingredients

1 cup (210 g) basmati rice
2 tbsp ghee
1 bay leaf
1" stick cinnamon
3-4 cloves
1 black cardamom
1 large onion, sliced
¾ tsp salt
1 tsp red chilli powder
½ tsp garam masala powder

Method

1. Wash and soak the rice in water for half an hour.
2. Heat the ghee in a heavy-bottomed pan. Fry the whole spices for a few seconds and add the sliced onions. Sauté over medium heat for 8-10 minutes until the onions are browned.
3. To this, add the drained rice, salt and red chilli powder. Sauté gently for 1-2 minutes.
4. Add 1½ cups of water to the rice and bring to a boil over high heat.
5. Reduce the heat, cover and cook for 7-8 minutes until all the water is absorbed and the rice is cooked. Sprinkle garam masala powder and stir gently to combine.
6. Transfer into a serving bowl and serve with Sindhi saibhaji (page 174).

Sweets

Til Chikki

Sesame Seed Praline

TIME TAKEN: 25 MINUTES

Tilgul ghya, goad, goad bola (eat til gul and talk sweet) is how people in Maharashtra greet each with sesame seed laddoos on the eve of Sankranti. Sesame seeds make a grand appearance in January in most parts of India, around the time of Makar Sankranti, as the sun moves into the zodiac of Capricorn. Up north and in the west, it assumes the forms of laddoo, chikki, revdi, and gajak. In Punjab, they also go by the name of til pinni. Til pitha and tilor laru are prepared in Assam for Bihu, celebrated around the same time. This is a recipe for a basic chikki made using sesame seeds. Stock up on this for your sweet cravings in the winters.

Ingredients

1¼ cups (170 g) white sesame seeds
1 cup (150 g) chopped jaggery
1 tsp ghee
2-3 tsp ghee to grease tray

Method

1. Heat a pan over medium heat. Add the white sesame seeds and toast until they start popping. Remove the toasted sesame seeds to a plate and keep aside.
2. Keep a silicone mat greased with some ghee ready.
3. In the same pan, add the chopped jaggery and allow it to melt. Once the jaggery has melted, reduce the heat and allow it to simmer. Keep a small cup of water handy.
4. After 4-5 minutes of simmering, the top layer of the jaggery will look shiny. Put a few drops of jaggery in the cup of water. You should be able to roll the water cooled melted jaggery into a ball. When you drop the ball in a cup or on the counter, it will make a sharp sound indicating that the caramel is ready for the praline.
5. Remove from the heat and mix in the toasted sesame seeds, working fast.
6. Transfer the mixture to the silicone mat. Using a greased rolling pin, roll this mixture into a very thin layer.
7. Using a pizza cutter, cut into shards or pieces, and save in an airtight container.

- *When buying jaggery, ensure that it is the variety to make chikki, which gives a glossy crisp finish.*
- *If you have a candy thermometer, the temperature of the caramel should be around 160-180°C (320-360 F) when you remove it from heat.*
- *The rolled out layer of praline when still hot can be wrapped around a cup or bowl greased with some ghee on the outside. Once cooled, it can be removed to get a chikki bowl.*

Sandesh

Bengali Cottage Cheese Dessert

TIME TAKEN: 40 MINUTES | MAKES 12 PIECES

Sandesh is prepared using only two ingredients – chenna (cottage cheese) and sugar. However, there are multiple variations of this popular Bengali sweet – from nolen gurer sandesh, sweetened with date palm jaggery to seasonal fruits like mangoes and strawberries.

Ingredients

1 litre full cream milk
Juice of 1 lime
½ cup (100 g) finely chopped strawberries
3 tbsp powdered sugar
3-4 strawberries (for garnish)
Mint leaves (for garnish, optional)

Method

1. To make the chenna (cheese), pour the milk into a saucepan and heat until it comes up to a boil. Reduce the heat and stir in the lemon juice. Continue stirring until the milk separates into solids and whey. The solid component is the cheese / chenna / paneer.
2. Pass this through a muslin lined sieve and wash the cheese under running water to stop it from cooking further and to remove any traces of sourness from the lemon juice. Tie the ends of the muslin cloth and drain for 15 minutes.
3. Meanwhile, in a small saucepan, combine chopped strawberries with powdered sugar and 2 tablespoon of water. Bring this to a boil and allow to simmer over low heat for around 8-10 minutes until you get a strawberry preserve.
4. Remove the drained cheese into a bowl and knead it for 5-6 minutes until it is of a smooth texture. This can also be done in the food processor.
5. Add the strawberry preserve and continue kneading for 4-5 minutes until it is well incorporated into the cheese. Cover and refrigerate for one hour.
6. Divide into 12 portions and shape into rounds. Place a thin slice of strawberry over each piece and garnish with a small mint leaf.

- *Sandesh moulds are popular in West Bengal where the prepared cheese mixture is pressed in and given beautiful, artistic shapes. If you have a cookie mould or something similar, you could use that as well to shape the sandesh.*
- *Keep the sandesh in an airtight box in the refrigerator and consume within 24 hours.*
- *The prepared strawberry puree can be frozen and used to prepare the sandesh when the berries are not in season. Thaw a cube of the puree in the microwave and then proceed with the recipe.*
- *You can also make strawberry sandesh with a strawberry preserve that has a high percentage of fruit content, in case the fruit is not in season.*

Rajgira Halwa / Sheera

Amaranth Flour Fudge

TIME TAKEN: 25 MINUTES | SERVES 4

Amaranth flour or rajgira is one of the many naturally gluten-free flours used in Indian cuisine. Amaranth being a pseudo grain, it is one of the ingredients allowed to be consumed even during (religious) fasts, as against wheat and rice, both of which are not allowed. The deep nutty flavour of the flour is enhanced by slow roasting in ghee. Serve this minimalist halva as a part of your next festive Indian thali.

Ingredients

1 cup (100 g) amaranth flour
½ cup (100 g) ghee
½ cup (100 g) sugar

FOR GARNISH
1 tbsp chopped pistachios
1 tbsp chopped almonds
1 tbsp chopped cashews
1 tsp dried rose petals

Method

1. In a heavy-bottomed pan, mix the flour and ghee. Roast it over low to medium heat for 7-8 minutes until the flour is aromatic and turns a few shades darker to a light brown colour.
2. Heat 200 ml water on the side in a saucepan. To the well roasted flour–ghee mixture in the pan, add the hot water carefully with constant stirring. The water will get absorbed almost immediately.
3. Add the sugar to the mixture and keep stirring for around 5 minutes. The sugar will dissolve and combine into the halva and the ghee will start separating out. Turn off the heat, cover and keep for 10 minutes.
4. Garnish with a mixture of chopped nuts and dried rose petals. Serve hot.

Chenna Poda

Indian Cheesecake from Odisha

TIME TAKEN: 45 MINUTES | SERVES 6

Chenna poda is a traditional sweet from the eastern state of Odisha. What it lacks in limelight, it more than makes up for in the taste department. Chenna poda is made using paneer (chenna) and traditionally baked over a log fire for a few hours. A layer of caramel at the bottom gives it the burnished colour and the slightly bitter caramel flavour to the cake that just sets it apart from any other Indian sweet.

Ingredients

2 tbsp ghee, divided

2 tbsp cashew nut pieces

2 tbsp raisins

200-250 grams paneer (fresh homemade paneer is best)

½ cup (100 g) granulated sugar

½ tsp ground green cardamom

1 tbsp fine semolina (chiroti rava)

1-2 tbsp milk (optional)

Method

1. Preheat the oven at 180°C.
2. Heat 1 tbsp ghee in a small pan and fry the cashew nut bits until golden brown. Remove with a spoon and keep aside. Fry the raisins in the remaining ghee until puffed up. Keep this along with the fried cashews.
3. Grease a 5-6 inch round pudding mould or cake tin with ghee. Sprinkle 2 tbsp of sugar in the tin and hold it with a pair of tongs over medium heat. Keep swirling the sugar as it melts and caramelizes so that the caramel coats the bottom of the tin.
4. In a food processor, combine the crumbled paneer, sugar, ground green cardamom, and rava. Blend to a smooth paste. Use 1-2 tbsp of milk if the mixture is very dry.
5. Remove this paste into a bowl. Combine with the fried cashews and raisins.
6. Transfer this over the caramel layer in the prepared tin.
7. Bake in the preheated oven at 180°C for 25 minutes until a skewer comes out clean and the top is a dark golden brown.
8. Allow the chenna poda to cool in the tin for an hour. Run a knife around the sides, loosening the cake from the tin. Turn over into a dish and cut into wedges or pieces. Serve warm.

- *When making paneer at home for this dish, do not squeeze out all the whey. A bit of extra moisture in the paneer prevents the cake from drying out in the oven.*
- *To make this gluten free, almond or coconut flour can be used instead of rava.*
- *Cashews fried in ghee and raisins add texture to this soft cake, but you can also make a plain chenna poda with just paneer, sugar, and rava.*

Holige

Sweet Flatbread

TIME TAKEN: 5 HOURS, INCLUDING SOAKING TIME | MAKES 8

These sweet stuffed 'rotis' are made in different parts of India during the festival of Sankranti, around the time of winter harvest. Called puranpoli in Maharashtra and Gujarat, boli in Tamil Nadu, bobbatlu in Andhra cuisine, and holige or obbattu in Karnataka, each community prepares this dish differently.

Ingredients

FOR FILLING

1 cup (200 g) Bengal gram (chana dal)
2 cups (300 g) powdered/crushed jaggery
1 tsp green cardamom powder / 4 pieces

FOR DOUGH

2 cups (220 g) all-purpose flour
1 cup (200 g) fine semolina (chiroti rava)
½ tsp ground turmeric
½ tsp salt
¼ cup (60 ml) milk
6 tbsp vegetable oil or coconut oil
Ghee, for cooking

Method

1. Wash and soak chana dal for 2 hours. Drain well and combine with 5 cups of water and bring to a boil. Do not cover the vessel. Boil for around 30-40 minutes until the lentils are soft but not mushy. Drain by passing through a sieve and let it drain completely for 15 minutes.
2. While the dal is still hot, add the jaggery. Add green cardamom powder. Simmer until the liquid is dried out.
3. Allow to cool. Grind in a mixer to a fine paste. Remove to a dish and divide into 50 gram portions, roll into balls. Keep this covered with a damp cloth in the fridge until ready to use.
4. To make the covering dough, mix the flour, semolina, turmeric and salt in a bowl. Add enough water to make a loose dough. Add milk and knead. Add 2 tablespoon oil and knead well for 5 minutes. Make into a ball. Apply a layer of oil on top and let it rest in a covered bowl for 2 hours.
5. Take the remaining oil and add it to the dough in batches, kneading and incorporating the oil into the dough well. Divide the dough into 75 gram portions (around 8 balls). This dough is smooth enough to spread with your hands using a cling film or a parchment paper.
6. Take each ball of sweet filling. Place it in the disc of dough and wrap the dough around the filling. Roll between palms until smooth.
7. Flatten this disc on a piece of parchment paper. Use your fingers to flatter further.
8. You can completely spread out using your fingers until you get a 7-8" thin flat holige. You can also partly spread out with hands and then use a rolling pin to spread out thinly.
9. Transfer onto a hot skillet with the aid of the parchment paper. Peel off the paper once the holige is somewhat stuck to the skillet. Use the same paper to prepare the next one.
10. Once golden spots appear, turn over. Apply ghee and let the other side cook for a minute over medium heat until cooked.
11. Remove from the heat and serve hot along with some ghee for dipping.

Index

Acknowledgements

A project like this is a result of the efforts, dedication
and support of a number of people.

I am thankful to Priya Kapoor and Chirag Thakkar at Roli Books
for approaching me with this idea of a beautiful vegetarian
cookbook showcasing recipes from around India and
seeing this book through.

The entire team at Roli Books ensure that each of
their books is a delight to the reader.

Friends who are gifted cooks, Bivarani Ngangom and
Mallika Parikh, for sharing their family recipes of Manipuri
black rice kheer and rajgira halwa respectively.

My son, who always cheered me up with his puns or calmed
me down by giving me a talk when I was snowed over by
book work and stressed over deadlines.

ISBN: 9789392130434

© Roli Books 2022
© Text and recipes, Nandita Iyer

Published in India by Roli Books
M-75, Greater Kailash II Market
New Delhi-110 048, India
Phone: ++91-11-40682000
Email: info@rolibooks.com
Website: www.rolibooks.com

Editors: Priya Kapoor, Neelam Narula
Illustrations: Abhilasha Dewan, Anita Verma
Design: Sneha Pamneja
Pre-press: Jyoti Dey
Production: Lavinia Rao

Printed and bound in India by
Naveen Printers, New Delhi